Mastering Networking

Mastering Networking

Forge Your Own Career Opportunities

Richard Cogswell

BEP

BUSINESS EXPERT PRESS

Leader in applied, concise business books

First published in 2025 by
Business Expert Press, LLC
222 East 46th Street, New York, NY 10017
www.businessexpertpress.com

ISBN-13: 978-1-63742-874-0 (paperback)
ISBN-13: 978-1-63742-875-7 (e-book)

Business Career Development Collection

First edition: 2025

10 9 8 7 6 5 4 3 2 1

EU SAFETY REPRESENTATIVE
Mare Nostrum Group B.V.
Mauritskade 21D
1091 GC Amsterdam
The Netherlands
gpsr@mare-nostrum.co.uk

To: Jack, Cady, Emma
May you grow curious, courageous and kind.
May you always walk boldly towards the life you imagine.

Description

The Game Is Not Rigged, the Game Has Changed

This is a book for anyone currently going through the lonely, difficult, and mostly demoralizing hunt for work in today's online world. Whether you are looking for something new, something better, or indeed something at all, this book provides tools and techniques to better your chances of achieving what you deserve, faster.

Anyone already in the job market will already know why you need this. Today's candidate experience is fundamentally broken. The recruitment industry has undergone incredible change and is honestly misunderstood by candidates today. Expectations do not meet the experienced reality, which is for the most part frustrating and subpar. In the digital age, numerous channels have emerged to support recruitment, however, these platforms often fail to provide jobseekers confidence that their efforts will lead to the results they want.

The honest truth is that finding job opportunities, whatever your circumstances, is tough, and harder still to manage should you find yourself currently out of work and facing unexpected economic pressures. We will explore the reasons for all of this throughout this book because it is important to know the landscape to be able to consider changing approaches to improve your fortunes. When you are better informed, better equipped, and guided by a clearer map, your journey becomes not only smoother, but far more successful.

My goal is to help you to avoid missteps and false turns. This is a book about how to take back control of your candidacy and how to maximize your chances of getting the job that you desire without total reliance on the recruitment industry. It will still take time, it will still take a lot of work, and you will still need to consider your energy and mental health, however, within the coming chapters, you will learn how to create your own job opportunities and how to maximize your chances of success when you are in an interview process. Differentiation is the key because most candidates do not take control of the recruitment or interview process at all. In fact, the lack of research done by candidates, in general, is frankly staggering. This book will help you put yourself in pole position compared to the rest of the application pack.

Hard Work and a Change of Mindset

There is a hard lesson to be learned, if you want to get to where you are going and if you do not like your present circumstances and results, no one is going to give you anything unless you work for it. This will require of you, research, practice, applied networking, and perhaps even fundamental changes of perspective and mindset. Not everyone is comfortable or adept at self-promotion, and this book will help you to take on these challenges and will help you to overcome any fear and inertia you might be experiencing.

It may be hard, and it may take time, but believe me it will be worth it. The destination is the key. Once you get there, the journey will have been worth the hardships. The achievement of your goal will be more pleasurable and impactful precisely because you made it all happen. It will help form and shape you. It will give you greater perspective and courage as well as the tools to be better in your job and within life in general. Self-promotion and networking are muscles that only improve with use.

Bold claims? Not if you take the lessons of this book to heart and practice them. Networking, for example, is not something you should be focusing on only when needed. Too many turn to networking as a solution only when it is too late. The tools and techniques to develop and honor a professional network, one that will sustain and help develop you are all contained within.

We will discuss the reasons why people are reticent to put themselves out there more and market themselves better, but, as with anything, you must take the first steps. This takes courage, but, provided you take on the approaches suggested within, you will soon gain confidence because you can in truth get the attention of anyone. People are often reticent to reach out to strangers or senior professionals in their network due to fear of rejection, self-doubt, or concerns about being perceived as intrusive or opportunistic. The truth is that most will respond with kindness and assistance, provided that you are passionate, succinct, compelling, and make your requests clear and actionable. This does require a developed use of your emotional intelligence (EQ), of course, including a sense of never outstaying your welcome. This includes knowing when to walk away, but the point holds. Your network is there to help and sustain you.

The Connected Job Market

I will focus on what I call the "Connected Job Market." You may not realize it, but you are, right now, mere steps away from unpublished job opportunities, which could transform your career and your life. The challenge is that these opportunities are not advertised and are not serviced by the industry we all usually turn to when seeking alternative opportunities. Instead, we must actively find them and, as actively, pursue them. To do this, many will also have to change their approach to job hunting. Approaching people in compelling ways, creating dialogue, becoming a better networker and servant to one's community, creating and sustaining a brand, these are all ways to put yourself in the shop window, enabling you to be better identified for positions. For some, sales, promotion, and branding, are all dirty words. They need not be, provided that you are in the business of creating and demonstrating value. What these opportunities have in common is a need to bypass traditional recruitment channels entirely, at least as a first step. That means leading with the value that you can bring to others.

Why Make Any Change?

When you are applying, every opening can seem like a precious commodity. It should be expected that competition for roles should and will be high, even more so these days. However, when you encounter processes being abruptly closed and receive impersonal, automated rejection emails, it can easily feel like the game is rigged. This is a book about resetting the playing field. It is written for candidates to help them find their own career openings and to load the dice on their applications. It's about understanding why this is necessary in today's job market. It is about ensuring that you are well positioned to be spotted by the modern-day recruitment industry and candidate-sourcing techniques. It's about good and thorough preparation, so that when an opening or opportunity does present itself, you are more confident and ready to ensure that you make it to the next phase of the conversation. It's about acknowledging that you will likely have a panel interview and how to gain and maintain momentum throughout that process, right up to getting the contract for hire.

If you are still unconvinced, reflect on your current experiences of being a candidate. Let me guess what that has been like, and what you have likely experienced. Guaranteed, you have had long and complicated application processes, the type of experience that can deter candidates, especially when they are required to upload their résumé and then manually input the same details again and again into an Application Tracking System (ATS).

You will have been further frustrated by the lack of feedback from these same systems and from employers. You will have often felt, as the applicant, as if you are in the dark about whether an opportunity you have applied for is still open, let alone why you weren't selected, or what you could improve for the next time. Finally, you have to deal with the monotony and discouragement of your daily experience, making the entire thing feel like a demoralizing, uphill battle.

Such an impersonal and seemingly random experience can impact candidates when they are suddenly approached for a screening call, or an interview. Some may be overly nervous or under-practiced in such environments when suddenly present with them, especially if one is out of work and the stakes are higher than normal. Others may not be well prepared to understand the company or opportunity presented and, therefore, may not sell their experiences and qualities adequately. Within a flash, the opportunity is passed, and the forlorn waiting game continues.

There Is a Better Way

Recruitment is a conversation, application processes are not.

I am not saying that you should never again apply online through LinkedIn or elsewhere, far from it, continue to select and apply to roles that appeal to you, but do be conscious of what you are doing. Do not use this as your only approach. If you are not thinking how to get into direct hiring conversations and then leading the direction of the process as much as possible, then you are not going to maximize your chances. To be clear, this is not about dominating or being aggressive, but it is about being more "sales" minded. Perhaps some of you will be reacting to the word "sales" in this context. We will discuss this in detail. I think of sales as the process of essentially helping others. It is important that you develop your philosophy and understanding of what sales really is. This book might necessitate that you develop a different relationship with sales as a result.

How are you helping in the context of a recruitment process? You are here to help the hiring company make the right decision. Your role is to demonstrate that you have the skills, experiences, philosophies, and behaviors that will help solve the challenges of the organization and drive its success. A conversation is about how to put this across in a compelling, story-driven style. It is also about framing a two-way, mutually beneficial exchange. This book will not only help you better your chances in the new "traditional" way of applying for jobs online, it will also help you in any interview processes you might find yourself in. More particularly, it will help you increase the opportunity for you to be hired for the roles you really want within a process that is more geared and focused toward your success. What have you got to lose? You already know what doing the same thing will get you.

We've reviewed your background and experience, and, unfortunately, we have decided to move ahead with other candidates. We appreciate the time you took to apply and encourage you not to let this be the end of your exploration of careers at [company.]

Remember, the status quo remains and is waiting for you right now. You can always go back to answering hundreds of job adverts from which you will likely receive only few responses, if at all. You can go back to a process designed in such a way that the recruiters probably do not even look at your application and, if they do, are screening it in moments. You will have the soul-sucking promise of endless reentering of your submitted curriculum vitae (CV), details into an appalling candidate management system, even if you have previously applied to this organization. You can go back to the system-generated email acknowledgments or rejections. This already awaits you, now is the time to try something new and now is the time to "break the recruitment process."

Support

This is also a book about support. Support for anyone working their way through the often lonely and isolating experience of job hunting. I want you to know that we all have been through what you are today experiencing and that we are there for you, rooting for you to win!

Key Topics

- **Understanding the Recruitment Industry:** What has changed? How does it work? How does one optimize their relationship with the industry?
- **Selling and Promoting Your Value:** Understanding what it means to think in terms of "sales" and how to focus on the "return on investment" (ROI), that you bring.
- **Personal Brand and Values:** Learn how to differentiate through the creation of a personal brand based on your values and approaches.
- **Networking:** How to network effectively and how to be a good servant to your network. How networking can enable you to create your own job opportunities. How your network can help you differentiate in interview and ensure that you make the greatest possible impacts and ROI once you are in the role you have applied for.
- **Research and Preparation:** Learn research techniques to help you identify the hiring manager and learn all you can about them and the company you are interviewing for.
- **Templates to Take Control:** Find templates to help you create deeper dialogue with hiring managers. Learn how you might control the conversation and increase differentiation from other candidates.
- **Resilience and Healthy Habits:** Getting recruited takes time, especially if you are in a poor hiring environment or if you are a mid-to-senior hire. Many markets globally are still in what might be called "The Great Hesitation," post-COVID, in the sense that investment in hiring has not returned to pre-pandemic levels. Learn how to focus on your mental health so that you might prevail intact.

Contents

List of Figures

Foreword

> **Chapter Summary**
> - The internet forever changed the recruitment industry.
> - "Traditional" recruitment, meeting and fronting candidates, has never recovered. Be more aware of the process you are entering.
> - The "Connected Job Market" and how it might make a difference for your job search.

On reflection, the modern-day candidate experience, which is the gateway for most to the recruitment industry and to getting hired, is like dealing with a machine.

Since becoming an author, I have become more active on LinkedIn, especially in terms of using its publishing tools to post content and bring an audience to my work. In the course of this, I have noticed that there are so many posts about job hunting. Most focus on poor candidate experiences. They do not make happy reading. They are published by recruiters and candidates alike, and they all hit a nerve, they are some of the most interacted with posts out there. One I saw recently had well over 8,000 interactions and hundreds of reposts. That should tell you something. The modern-day recruitment experience is, for the most part, universally bad, which is why these posts are so emotive and drawing such volumes of reaction.

Mostly these conversations are about the length of time recruitment takes or negative stories illustrating the frustrations of the candidate experience, which is almost uniformly woeful. On reflection, the modern-day candidate experience is like dealing with an unseen, uncaring machine. Machines have no emotions, machines excel at processing multiple thousands of mundane calculations but lack compassion. Recruitment used to be about humanity, and for many in the business it still is. Recruitment is filled with sincere, passionate, and mission-driven individuals, I know many personally, but the industry was so fundamentally changed by the internet that not only have the majority of recruiter's roles and focuses shifted, but the candidate expectation of the industry has not caught up to the present reality.

What is truly disheartening in all of this is that candidates expect the process to be different. They don't understand why the industry has shifted, nor do they know how to change their outcomes. In reality, even those of us who aim to "break the recruitment cycle" often fall back into the habit of submitting hundreds of applications, only to see a meager 2 percent return on the significant time, energy, creativity, and mental resilience invested.

Work in a Better Way

I have a long career behind, and I hope ahead of me still. I have been fortunate to have been headhunted multiple times, but I also created my own job opportunities five times. On these occasions, I created the opportunity that I was then hired for. I have also been made redundant, four times so far, and twice have had extended periods out of work and on the job hunt. One of those times lasted almost a year during a poor recruitment market. I have also spent a couple of years in the recruitment industry, albeit not as a recruiter myself, that said, I did experience deep insights into that industry and how it functions today. I have also hired many people over the years and have something to say about how candidates choose to turn up and represent themselves at interview. As a candidate I have bypassed recruiters who initially rejected me to gain interviews, and I have taken control of the majority of interview processes I have had over the years. Learning how to differentiate will get you the roles you deserve. I am also as prone to fear and inertia as anyone, in spite of being very practiced at networking and cold outreach. These emotions and feelings are old friends indeed.

I have been there, I have been the frustrated candidate, and I have experienced the slog of trying to work within a process that is not optimized to see you, the candidate, or allow you the opportunity to show what you could bring to an advertised role. I have ventured outside of my industry on a number of occasions and have then become confusing to the modern-day recruiter, who is only used to seeing candidates from firms they recognize. I have also applied for many roles that seemingly are out there, open and available, but in truth are not.

To accept any change, one has to reflect and accept the truth one is being shown. Real lasting change requires a high level of commitment and self-motivation. All of us are at some point in the job market as candidates. If you have come to accept the truth that the model is not working, then I hope you have found your way to this book, and I hope it provides some approaches that can help you navigate the new realities while bolstering your resilience and mental health at the same time. The techniques within will sustain you not only in your career but also in life, wherever that may take you.

Some LinkedIn Truths

The fact that a role is posted does not mean that everyone reasonably qualified has a shot at it. Due to the impact the digital revolution has had on recruitment, all of us candidates are forced down the path of using the largest job boards and platforms to respond to job advertisements. Hence, within this book, we will discuss LinkedIn a great deal. There are other job boards and online platforms, yes, but globally LinkedIn is the most unique and largest professional online community, it has, quite simply, changed the game.

We have to talk about LinkedIn's good, bad, and the ugly. For the record, I have never worked there. I do have folks within my network from LinkedIn, but they have had no influence over anything I have written, which I have positioned from the perspective as a user, a content creator, an employee, a candidate, and someone who frankly has a love/hate thing going on with the platform.

As with any tool, there are good ways to work with it to maximize your outcomes, and there are the bad, which will serve to underplay your visibility in recruitment processes. To work well with LinkedIn and with the wider recruitment industry, it is important, and vital indeed, to know how it works and how best to use it for the greatest possible outcomes.

For us professionals who make up the LinkedIn community of users, and there are over a billion of us globally, it is primarily a publishing platform. On it you will find all manner of professional (and annoyingly, increasingly social) content. Opinions, thought leadership, and commentary from industry professionals are packed into your daily feed.

A Broken Candidate Experience

Let's face it, applying to jobs these days is often a horrible and frustrating process, it can feel like you are shipwrecked. You stand on your isolated, lonely shore forlornly throwing out messages in bottles awaiting some form of response. Very few come back at all. In addition, the messages are not at all helpful, "*Thank you for your application; we have decided to explore other candidates at this time,*" and yet the jobs you have applied for seemingly stay perpetually open and even if you have something to offer, you are not contacted. It's hard not to take it all personally. Not only is it a lonely experience, but it is also one that tests your resilience and fortitude to the max. It can all seem willfully cruel. You can be left with the impression that the process is not actually an open one at all (Figure 1).

Figure 1 The shipwrecked candidate

Understanding Recruitment

The truth is that there are several things at play that can prevent your candidacy from being seen at all. For a so-called people business, the majority of recruiters seem very hands-off when it comes to the candidate. If it is not the candidate, then who are they serving? The answer here is, simply put, their client, which is to say, the hiring company. Clients are the true focus of the mainstream recruitment industry because hiring "requisitions" are increasingly hard to find.

The modern-day recruiter is in a perpetual battle with clients who think they can directly attract talent in the marketplace. This is largely because today they have the same access to the same tools as recruiters do, and the perception is that it is cheaper for the hiring company to go it alone. This means the focus has become one of "ownership." Once a candidate is registered on a database, even if they have applied or not, a company can "claim them." That's lost revenue for the recruiter. So, the recruiter has to focus first, on getting a client to work with, second, manage their client, and third, ensure that any identified candidate is theirs, so they might bill for a placement. This type of pressure leads many traditional recruiters to focus on repeatable template hiring so that they can demonstrate an expertise through access to a talent network, while benefiting from sustainable bookings. This tends to lead traditional recruiters to high-demand roles, usually based around skills, such as development, compliance, finance, construction, or project management. That leaves many roles, particularly mid-to-senior leadership roles, out in the comparative cold, as they are deemed too hard to fill, too few, and too time-consuming for the recruiter, with no guarantee of commission.

In this sense, the candidates, in order for them to be better prepared, need to understand who they are engaged with, as not all recruiters are the same. Here we need to differentiate between the global players like Randstad, Manpower, Hays, Allegis, and the list goes on, and the niche players who differentiate through focus or approach, such as those focusing on confidential hires or headhunting.

Understand the beast and you can better adapt your approaches and mindset. For example, if you are applying for a role advertised by a mainstream agency, the more you know about how they work in general, the better you can already steel yourself in applying, and I do mean steel yourself, to not hearing back soon, or indeed ever, about your application. Critically, you can also then invest your time in other approaches and applications that will bring more fruitful returns.

This is really not intended as an "anti-Recruitment" treatise. I think it is an incredibly hard job and it is filled with passionate individuals, but this is a book about trying to not only help folks deal with something they find suboptimal, but to also provide tools and techniques to help them improve their outcomes.

The thing that we as candidates simply must do is to treat every posted role, no matter how perfect for us, with the utmost suspicion. Apply, but know that a posted job is actually very likely to have a preferred candidate already identified, it's just not you, nor is it ever likely to be you. This is what I mean when I say that you must look after your mindset.

Think of a physical trainer in the gym, should you have one, *they* will not inherently make you fitter, but *you will*, through *your* choices, *your* behaviors, and *your* energy and focus. All of this comes down to you, especially as you are the asset in this conversation, with your skills, experiences, and capacity to affect a role and a company's outcomes. Your ability to provide an ROI to the hiring organization is the quality we are looking to maximize as you approach the connected job market.

Takeaways

- *If you don't change, your results will remain the same.*
- *Recruitment and recruitment processes have fundamentally changed and not necessarily for the benefit of candidates. Understand why, so that you may adapt.*
- *Ask yourself if you are ready for change, ready to try new approaches, and if the answer is yes, read on, this journey is for you!*

CHAPTER 1

My Last Job Interview and "The Connected Job Market"

Chapter Summary

- The ways you get into hiring situations have changed.
- Do not be unconnected. Network, especially if you are not actively looking for work right now.
- Be conscious of when you might be the obstacle to getting into hiring situations.

Tapping the "Connected Job Market"

You are only, ever, a few connections away from your next career-changing conversation.

Five times in my career I have found employment through what I call the "Connected Job Market." The first time this happened I was alive to water-cooler talk in the office. The chatter was of a new entrant to the market, with exciting technological approaches and ambitions to open new markets beyond the one I was currently expert in. I spoke to a colleague who had met the founders and gained an email address. I emailed with an overview of my experience, and where I wanted to take them, I mentioned that my motivation was to grow and extend my expertise into new solutions concurrent with their phase 2 plans.

Very quickly, I was invited to meet the founders, they invited their development team to join the interview, and I was suddenly work-shopping the market needs, including how I would sell automated enterprise-level variations of their solution. We effectively designed the demo together and mapped out a go-to-market approach. My contract for hire was negotiated that very afternoon. Over the next 8 years, I would build two customer bases from scratch for two propositions, and then build the teams to face these markets and customers. This startup would end up being acquired by what is now Finastra, the second largest payments company on the planet. Through this company I would sell the solution that enabled me to see the world, and which brought me to Asia, beginning a completely new phase of my life and career journey. It was an amazing experience, which all started from an overheard conversation that I had been alive to.

Every time I have entered the connected job market, it has been a story of being alive to networking and opportunity, creating meetings through compelling sales pitches, and being able to define the focuses and impact I would deliver to a role. In all cases, these roles were subsequently advertised. In each of these environments, I had privileged access, enabling me to ask questions so that I could position my value in a way that no external candidate could. I built outcome-oriented connection. That can of course be done in a traditional interview process, and we will look at ways to do this, but it is substantially harder to do from the outside as opposed to being inside and shaping the hiring conversation.

None of these experiences were a one-off, there is a process to achieving this, and it works. When these roles were advertised, I was the shortlisted candidate. How did I achieve this? By directly utilizing my network as opposed to responding to job adverts. Critically, no recruiters or headhunters were involved. But it's not just about working your way into conversations that can lead to opportunities, it's about being visible to the right kind of recruiter. I have also been headhunted for two significant roles in my career so far. To be successfully headhunted, you need to be visible to the sourcing practices used by that type of recruiter, techniques I will also cover later.

It is my contention, and the purpose of this book, to show why these routes to employment are increasingly necessary to take and how to do it most effectively. This is especially the case for mid-to-senior roles, unless you are very specialized. You may not realize it now, but your next job opportunity, your next raise, your next promotion or advancement are already there, simply waiting for you to come find them.

The Use of Network in Recruitment

If you're looking for work and not tapping into your network as a first step, then you are missing out on one of the most powerful tools in your job search arsenal. Networking gives you access to the connected job market through referrals and insider knowledge. By reaching out to former colleagues, mentors, and industry contacts, you can gain valuable insights, recommendations, and even direct introductions to hiring managers. In a competitive job market, personal connections can be the key differentiator that will help you stand out and secure the role you are after.

I would be very hesitant when it comes to the topic of published statistics of those using their network as a first port of call during a job search. Simply put, the surveys or articles that suggest that 70 to 80 percent of candidates leverage their networks before turning to recruiters do not seem reliable, as they are based on LinkedIn user polls, which can only show a directional sense of the topic. This is because the sample size of those responding will be small. Instinctually, however, I would say that those in senior positions would likely use their network more than those in entry to midlevel positions. A senior leader will most likely have a more developed network, one they have served well, which would be willing and able to help them in the first steps of introducing interesting career conversations.

I would think for a huge swathe of job hunters, perhaps even the vast majority, that LinkedIn and other job boards will dominate in their job searches as a first port of call. Company websites will likely come next, and, finally, there may be some thought to reach out to their networks both social and professional, but there might be some reticence on their part to do so as well. Hesitation might come in the form of feeling that their network is underdeveloped, or that they don't know where to start or how to begin those conversations. We will go into this aspect in more detail with approaches and strategies to help you, as networking in this sense has to be proactive and direct.

The effectiveness of networking is underscored by the fact that many publicly advertised openings are actually filled through internal referrals.

Employers often encourage this by offering monetary bonuses to employees for successful referrals, this is essentially passing a smaller bonus to the employee rather than paying a sizable recruiter fee. This network-first approach is particularly prevalent in industries where personal relationships and recommendations are highly valued.

The Shortlisted Candidate

What does it mean to be the shortlisted candidate? It means that you have full knowledge of, and full access to, the hiring contingent of the company you are set to join. It means you have insider access to them, more time with them, and more chances to have deeper, more progressive discussions about what your contribution will look like, compared to those any external candidate could possibly have.

You will have a clear advantage over anyone coming late into this process, because they will have to start from scratch. Anyone new to the process will have to start cold, compared to you. They will not have any considerable knowledge about the company, the recruitment panel or the challenges, goals, expected outcomes, KPIs, and contribution targets associated with the position to which they have applied. Not only will they have to excel at doing their research but will also have to deliver an extraordinarily compelling ROI plan to be able to unseat the one you have already socialized and built alignment for, as part of your created hiring process. It's not impossible that someone could come on the outside to overtake you, but you have the clear inside lane within this process, you are the clear favorite.

Everyone else is outside the process looking in. The rest will be responding to a job advert, one they will have to interpret. Everyone else must fall back on the assumptions and research that they do to prepare for interview, and, as we will find out, most candidates really do little or no research at all when interviewing. It means that you will blow away 99 percent of those coming into the process through a public job posting.

Getting to this type of privileged job access still takes work, takes time, and you will still have to live through prolonged periods of no news or silence. In fact, those times may well be extended, because in this scenario the job is effectively being scoped by you through your discussions, so be prepared for longer periods with no update. Why? This is because, in these circumstances, the work of gaining budget, authority to hire, of involving all stakeholders and preparing a public advertisement of the role, of sourcing and interviewing other candidates as part of a "free and fair" process, takes time. Be prepared for a process that might take months but one that will ultimately pay off.

My Last Job Interview

Let me tell you about my last job interview. This is currently a live process, so by the time this is published, it may or may not be six times I have successfully navigated the connected job market. I hope it serves to illuminate many of the topics I have mentioned, and serves as a case study on how a connected job market interaction may go.

It all began with lunch with a colleague and friend. I meet him maybe three or four times a year, on this occasion, we were both attending a conference in Bangkok. I have spent the majority of my working life in an industry that is diverse in its players, and we were discussing the various propositions in the market, including their relative strengths and weaknesses. It was a great conversation, and lunch, given that we were in Bangkok was not bad either!

One of the biggest and most well-known companies in our industry's ecosystem was brought up. This company is one of the 50-pound gorillas. The conversation began to settle specifically around how this provider was something of an enigma in that they had all the attributes to dominate globally, and, yet, we could both observe from our respective positions as competitor and partner, that they were failing to do so. Our conversation settled into a discussion about why this might be the case. In spite of our coming from different perspectives, we were in complete alignment on the list of reasons why this player was not achieving what they should be.

We both agreed that while challenging, this position was eminently fixable, given the right hire, the right executive aircover, and someone motivated to turn this supertanker around. The footnote was that my friend was close to their head of commercial operations for the region. Indeed, he had also had many conversations over time with this executive about changing the dynamics of their business approach. Maybe this was someone motivated to look outside of their usual talent pool and sufficiently motivated to make the kind of changes we had been discussing?

Months later, I heard on the grapevine that this company was reaching out to individuals to interview them for a new "Head of Region" role. I checked the company "Careers" page, as well as the LinkedIn posts of the executives I knew, and found nothing was being advertised or promoted for wider engagement. This was frustrating, but, not at all unusual. High-stature companies in this position are adept at directing their "Talent Acquisition," (TA), to go and search for a particular type of candidate from particular companies.

When on the periphery of the connected job market, we have to make the extra effort to get noticed. There is no way to do this other than to go for the hiring executive directly. You simply cannot use the company's HR, they only know what they know. HR will simply shoot your application down or ignore it. I guarantee an approach to them, even if you get the right person, will result in a rejection. Why? Their brief is clear, and if you do not fit the search criteria, that is, if your CV does not show one of the three or four firms that they are expecting, they will drop you. It is literally that binary. You need the hiring executives to bring you into the process in these cases, there is simply no other way. They can impose on the HR and TAs, not the other way around.

An element that my friend and I had identified as a weakness was that this industry giant always hired from the same cloth, by which I mean, their candidate pool was surprisingly fixated on what you might call traditional sources. From a business perspective, this was incredibly non-diverse in terms of background. Being a bank, they essentially hired from organizations that some also perceive to be like banks. Large, complex, bureaucratic, and often highly matrixed environments. However, surprisingly for a commercial position, these people were not necessarily salespeople. For my friend and myself, as we might impolitely suggest, these were politicians, at worse order-takers, as opposed to candidates coming from "practitioner" backgrounds, who would be better able to speak to the realities of the market dynamics and opportunity. When there is a ready catchment pool for hiring, there can be a blind eye to where real and dynamic growth might come from. The safer thing can be to repeatedly hire from where previous candidates have come from. This can be a huge blocker.

So, at this point, I was frustrated as I was keen to put myself into a position to have a discussion. Not only did I want to test my theories, but I also felt that at this point of my career, the role was a challenge I would relish. Truthfully, knowing I was not from the usual mold was tempering my frustration, however, given the fact that there was always a good chance that my perspectives might fall on deaf ears, even if I did find an audience for my proposal. This is a point to bear in mind when qualifying opportunity for yourself. When approaching a company, it does pay to understand any "table stakes," so as not to waste your time. Be conscious and, as hard as it sounds, be receptive to such dynamics when choosing whether to try and engage. While wrong on so many levels, this can severely limit your chances as you will be battling an organization, unless there is a force for change embodied in either an individual executive, or an organizational mandate.

You must understand that only a hiring manager can change the hiring emphasis. This is why "networked research" is such a powerful element of your job search. Reaching out to people in your network who either work, or have worked, or are connected to folks at your target company, can help you gather information prior to your outreach. This is so important to both hone your approaches and ensure that you are not ultimately wasting your precious time.

I was still in a privileged position, having caught a glimpse of a process that was not in plain sight. I was comfortable in my existing position, successful though underutilized, but, equally, I did not have to be on LinkedIn every day looking for exit opportunities. I knew I might be rejected at first call for the cultural reasons already outlined. If the conversation changed nothing, then so be it, nothing ventured nothing gained. It would be an honest attempt. In authentic sales, one of the things we are striving to do, is to first understand whether indeed there is a sale to be made at all. We call this process qualification of the opportunity. The problem was I needed to somehow insert myself into the conversation, the question was, how?

Weeks later, a friend from my network asked to have a beer with me. She confided that she was up for an interview, and, you guessed it, at this very company. She approached me to help coach her for the role, as it was an environment in which she didn't have any direct experience. While she was familiar with the technology and mechanisms involved, she needed to understand the value proposition and go-to-market. Furthermore, she sought guidance on how to succeed and elevate the role. As I had spent part of my career engaging directly with customers who required these solutions, she had thought of seeking my inputs. What she did have was the right company on her CV. She was cut from the cloth the bank was comfortable with, as such, their TA had identified and approached her. I applauded her initiative, as she was actively leveraging her network to learn and prepare for interview and I was delighted to help.

I respected what my friend was doing, rather than going in underprepared, she had taken the initiative to speak to someone who could coach her. She was doing everything I would have done, and that I am advising you, the reader, to do. I offered my expertise freely and happily. I was excited for her, happy that she was getting this opportunity. It would be a significant move for her, should she be successful.

Still, I could not help but feel that I, or someone with my type of market experience, should be in the position she was. There was no way, however, that I was going to use her to get into the conversation. So I waited, this time, because of loyalty to my friend and to honor her initiative in reaching out to me in the first place. I think, as well, that this time my prevarication was partly because my friend did come from the pool from which this company usually picked candidates.

So it was confirmed, the hiring company was acting to type. This situation aside, there is a fine line between valuing your expertise, understanding its worth, and finding excuses for non-action. Learn how to listen to yourself and ask yourself why you are not taking steps or acting more directly to advance yourself into a conversation. Identify whatever is holding you back, be it fear, nervousness, lack of knowledge, someone's title or seniority, perceived loyalty, and so on. Once you have identified what you are feeling, you can then dig deeper to understand these barriers and weigh up the cost of inaction. In this way, you can frame your preparedness for action in a positive and goal-oriented light, allowing you to identify the next steps required to get into those potentially career, and life-changing, conversations that you deserve to be in.

Your experience is invaluable, never underestimate its worth. Don't let titles or seniority stop you from engaging in meaningful conversations. True leadership is grounded in shared wisdom, not status.

My friend reported that her interview had gone well but that there was some delay in the process. The hiring company was facing global challenges, which were well documented in the news at the time. As it happened, these delays forced her to look into alternative opportunities, one of which she subsequently took. The board, should I want to advance was now again open once more.

Change the Mindset and Change the Game

The risk you sense, the fear that is restraining you, might just be the only barrier stopping you from taking the best, most transformative steps toward changing your life and career for the better.

I will talk a lot about changing your candidate mindset. Even before my connection had reached out for coaching, something had been holding me back, and I am not usually at all reticent to put myself forward, having done so successfully professionally and personally many times. It just goes to show that many things can pull us back from activities or actions that would ultimately benefit us. Putting yourself out there is to risk rejection. It's true of job hunting, it's true of life, and it's true of love. (Figure 1.1).

Why are we more likely to take enormous personal risks for friendship and love, but not for work and life?

Dating and networking for job creation share many similarities because both involve building relationships, establishing trust, and finding mutual value. In dating, you seek compatibility and shared goals, just as in networking where you are looking for professional alignment and opportunities. Both processes require effort and patience, you will never

*Figure 1.1 **Putting yourself out there***

simply land a job or form a meaningful connection overnight. In both scenarios, authenticity is crucial, you simply cannot force connections, just as you cannot force love, but with the right approach a natural synergy can lead to long-term benefits, whether that's a lasting partnership or a rewarding job opportunity. Develop your EQ, never outstay your welcome, and know when to let go and walk away. Just as in dating, where first impressions matter, making a strong professional impression is key when networking.

We often fear talking to an attractive stranger because of the potential for rejection, which can feel like a blow to our self-esteem. The perceived attractiveness of the stranger amplifies this fear, as we may place them on a pedestal, assuming they are out of our league or that they hold more social power. This creates anxiety about being judged or not measuring up. Evolutionary psychology suggests that this fear is rooted in our need for social acceptance, as rejection could have had serious survival consequences in past times. Additionally, our minds often overestimate the risks and underestimate the rewards, making the idea of approaching someone new seem much scarier than it actually is.

Job networking and dating are similar when it comes to the fear of rejection because both involve putting yourself out there in a vulnerable way. In job networking, just like in dating, you risk being turned down, ignored, or judged, which can feel deeply personal. Whether you're asking someone for professional advice, a referral, or a job lead, the fear of not being taken seriously, or being seen as unworthy, can trigger the same insecurities that arise when approaching a romantic interest. In both scenarios, rejection feels like a direct reflection on your value whether it is professional or personal, which makes it harder to take the first step. This shared fear stems from our desire for validation, acceptance, and the avoidance of failure, leading to hesitation in reaching out, despite the potential benefits.

However, in both cases, putting yourself out there is the only way to open doors to new opportunities and experiences, to grow, and to ultimately find fulfilling success. When it comes job hunting, it is also a complete necessity. Even if you simply keep doing you are doing, which is to say applying and applying again online, eventually you will get a hit. What then? You are then called to interview, and the process of needing to compete, to show your differentiated values, in terms of selling and promoting yourself, begins. At some point, it is coming to get you, therefore it is better to be confronting and dealing with the fears upfront and in the process finding better opportunities while you are at it.

That said, some people are not comfortable with self-promotion, especially if there is not a clear "official" route forward. For many, that call to interview makes the whole thing legitimate. To hold back, however, is to not use all the tools and advantages available to you in order to place yourself in the shop window, therefore missing out on a whole world of hidden, self-creatable opportunity. You will also diminish the impact you will make in any interview you do get, as you will simply not be as match-fit, ready, and polished, as you would otherwise be.

What Is Worse? Fear of Rejection or What Might Have Been?

What could be worse than a rejection, or the scenario your playful mind might be conjuring of a social humiliation you ask? Well, for me that would be the gnawing itch of regret and, more specifically, that hateful sensation of "what if." Again, the correlation to dating is startling and informative. What if I had spoken to him or her? Why are some of us more likely to take social risks for love, than take social risks for life and work?

The Connected Conversation Continues

Let's check in with my progress toward my last interview. I was hesitating with many thoughts swimming around in my mind. I was frustrated within my current role, but it was a dead recruitment environment post-COVID. So I would find myself thinking often about the process I was now suspecting had passed me by. I was definitely beginning to have a case of the "what ifs." I had searched again on LinkedIn, but I could still not identify the hiring executive, and I did not want to send out approaches to the wrong folks. For some reason, I was still reticent to ask directly for an introduction, partly because my friend and I were working together, and he was a partner to my business. When we had left our lunch discussion all those months ago, I had hinted broadly by saying, "*I'd love to talk to them one day about this,*" but this hint had clearly not landed, I had not been direct enough.

I tried a roundabout approach. To be clear, this was kind of cowardly, a soft way of trying to progress this opening. I turned to another friend, a headhunter who worked with the company in question, thinking it could be a good way to be both introduced and endorsed for the role at the same time. If anything, all it added was more dependencies as I had to coach my friend in being able to make approaches. Still I tried, even though I was aware that this was another form of delay. Weeks went by, and my headhunter friend could not find his way into the topic, or to find the hiring executive either. Why should he have been able to? I should have left it at a conversation on whether he might know who the hiring manager might be. The moral of this story is that you simply must be direct when you have the opportunity to be.

I found myself at my desk one morning mulling over this experience. Then something happened, almost as if I had willed it to. My Bangkok lunch companion happened to WhatsApp me. He was sharing news about his recent promotion and was thanking me for being a supporter and a friend. We shared his joy and discussed his new position. Now I summoned the courage to ask him if he knew whether the role I wanted was still open and whether he would mind introducing me to his contact for a coffee. He was happy to. Before I knew it introduction emails had been sent:

> *Hi [contact's name], a good business partner and friend of mine, Richard Cogswell could be a great fit for the current B2B opening. If you want to meet over a coffee, he's got some good ideas that he's willing to share regarding supply chain and other opportunities. He's got a plethora of experience. I'll drop out from here, just wanted to make the introduction. Cheers…*

With this, a date was quickly set to meet for a quick half-hour coffee. The game was suddenly afoot. Now I really did feel some pangs, was the role still open? Why had I not moved quicker? Still, this was an exciting breakthrough. However, if I was to discover that someone else was already shortlisted or hired, I knew I would regret my delay a great deal, but the point was that I now had a moment to prepare for and to attempt to maximize.

I prepped diligently and went to the meeting with a sense of excitement and nothing to lose. I went with the pure and specific goal of simply getting to the next conversation within this organization. The meeting went well. The hiring manager told me openly about the role, what he was looking for, why he had been struggling to find the right candidates, as well as what the role entailed. He also told me what the next steps would look like. He then told me that two candidates were already in the process and that he would have to speak with his boss about whether I could join so late in. He also confirmed that if she said yes, he was keen for me to be involved in the process.

At the time of writing, this process was again stalled due to the same global issues affecting hiring budgets at this company. The tale is I feel still instructive as it shows that to network your way into roles you must always confront feelings of inadequacy or fear, even if like me you have actually done it many times over. On this occasion, I was lucky, my delay did not harm me within the process. My point here is that delaying based upon fear or inertia will mostly result in lost opportunity. Once you have a lead, follow it up and strike early. Yes, there could be reasons why the process will not proceed or conclude right now, but you can relax knowing that you are in the minds of those who matter. You will have staked your claim.

Looking for Your Next Role, Even When You Do Not Have to

If my story should illustrate anything, it is that you should always back yourself. Prepare hard. Be compelling and add value. Serve your network and community. Do not delay. Do not let your fear or imagined scenarios stop you. It is good to feel nervousness, this means you care and means you are more likely to prepare a great outreach. Jump anyway. Get yourself into the position to be considered.

If you try and fail, nothing ventured, nothing gained. If you do get in the conversation, de-pressure yourself by acknowledging your victory in getting to a dialogue and focus on that exchange only for now. You will never regret being in a situation that could lead to an outcome when you have created it for yourself. Either way, you will learn so much more than sitting at the desk and regretting inaction. So what if it goes nowhere? You will have exercised an important skill, one that will pay off when you create the right conversation.

The point is that I have an active conversation in the market during a hiring downturn. It may or may not come to anything, as timing is everything. Meantime, I have been exercising skills and techniques that will sustain me should I suddenly find myself facing a situation of having to actively consider my next role. I know so many people who have been caught cold by a retrenchment or restructure. What all of these good, experienced folks had in common was the prospect of a standing start in respect to what to do about their sudden newly found situation. This can lead to a sensation of not knowing where to start or who to turn to. Creating compelling outreach is a muscle that must be trained and toned.

I have created job openings five times, this is not a fluke, and it's a process like any other. If I have done it, you can most certainly do it as well.

The Connected Job Market in Action

My story is the connected job market in action. Being receptive to conversations, especially chance ones, can lead to opportunity. It is wrong to speak of a "hidden" job market, there's nothing hidden about it. Hidden implies that something is deliberately or naturally concealed, often implying exclusivity or secrecy. The connected job market is discoverable. To discover it requires effort, creating access that others do not have.

The connected job market consists of roles filled through word-of-mouth recommendations, internal promotions, executive search firms, and proactive outreach by jobseekers to companies.

For jobseekers, this means adopting a more proactive approach while still leveraging job boards. Success in today's job market is about maximizing opportunities and expanding the scope of possibilities for securing a promotion or career move. Modern jobseekers must invest time and effort into networking, building professional relationships, and directly engaging with companies of interest to tap into the connected job market. Choosing not to do so is a conscious decision, similar to opting out of social media and being "offline." In the same way, a passive approach to job hunting leaves one thoroughly "unconnected." Being truly connected means you are just a few meaningful connections away from opportunity.

Takeaways

- *Be receptive to conversations that can lead to opportunities.*
- *Beware of procrastination, fear, or inertia. Always back yourself. Prepare hard. Be compelling and add value. Be bold. Do not be afraid.*
- *Serve your network and community.*
- *If you try and fail, then nothing ventured, nothing gained. Inertia is the killer of progress.*
- *Think about the value you can provide and put yourself in the shoes of the target. If you were them and there was a possibility to learn new approaches, would you not take it? What's to lose? Half-an-hour of time over a coffee is the only investment.*

- *Increase the privilege of your position, get to social conversations, get invited to meet others in the recruitment process, test your assumptions, and work on your thesis for hire.*
- *Once you get into a conversation, ensure you are ready, prepared, and know your goals. These are rare and important moments, do not waste them by simply turning up.*

CHAPTER 2

Recruitment:
A Changed Industry

Chapter Summary

- The recruitment industry was irrevocably transformed by the advent of the internet.
- LinkedIn can really be defined as a tool for the recruitment industry, for the rest of us, the candidates, it should be viewed as primarily a networking tool, a publishing platform, or a vehicle from which to advertise and sell services.
- Understand the phenomenon of sourcing centers and pre-screening techniques.
- Do not apply to LinkedIn job adverts assuming that they are open processes, teach yourself to approach hiring managers directly, whether applying to adverts or not.
- Research suggests that up to 75% of applications are filtered out by ATS before reaching a human reviewer. While factors like job criteria and hiring briefs play a role, overly designed, non-standard CV formats can also reduce your chances of making it through initial screening. Do not use fancy CV templates.
- While AI promises an improvement in the candidate and recruitment experience, do not rely on it to help you secure more work opportunity. AI will never supplant networking and sustained self-promotion in the connected job market.

The Recruitment Conundrum

Insanity is doing the same thing over and over and expecting different results.

Attributed to Albert Einstein

To understand why we need to change our approaches, we need to understand why the current recruitment environment is not best serving us. I evidence the truth of posts on LinkedIn detailing just how hard it is for candidates in the world of a changed recruitment industry (Figure 2.1).

The example shown below really hit a nerve, with a staggering level of engagement. As many as 22,763 people had read this post at the time I found it, a further 1,290 had taken the time to contribute comments, and 698 had reposted. No doubt more have since added to the conversation. It is not surprising to me that this post resonated, not only does it speak the truth in terms of the candidate experience, but it is really illustrating the fact that to stand any chance you must change the dynamic.

I spoke with a jobseeker friend who applied for 240 jobs on LinkedIn. He only selected job postings that were no more than 7 days old.

Surprisingly, 218 of his applications were not viewed by the recruiters who posted them.

The remaining 22 applications were also a disappointment, with 80% receiving an automatic rejection within a few minutes of applying.

He managed to get 3 interviews:

- An automated online chat from which he never heard back.
- A phone screening with a junior recruiter who wasn't prepared for the interview.
- An interview with a panel of 3 people. He made a good first impression and got to the second round, only to be ghosted after that.

Stop wasting people's time and fix the hiring process once and for all

Figure 2.1 LinkedIn recruitment post example

Source: Taken from a published LinkedIn post

I commented on the post, saying that in truth, most of these advertised jobs would likely have a shortlisted candidate behind them. It is important to understand where the value lies as a candidate and to then use LinkedIn to your advantage. If you do not, you will simply continue to lob arrows into the darkness, with no idea what, if anything, you are hitting. Unfortunately, for most candidates, LinkedIn is viewed as the default and most accessible path to what they believe are open and fair opportunities for available roles. If this is your mindset, then you are in for a very demoralizing and lonely journey. Be prepared for the experience described in the post, with over 200 applications leading to only a handful of interviews.

In large part, the problem is trust. Candidates feel let down because the perception is that recruitment is better than this. They also feel let down because the "legitimate" pathways to roles are such a disappointment. In my own LinkedIn survey, 56 percent of respondents reported that the most frustrating element of job hunting is the lack of feedback. Recruitment is a people business, but people have in many ways been taken out of recruitment. The perception is that someone, somewhere, is diligently reading all applications and working to elevate those who fit the skills and experiences needed. Truth is, there are huge amounts of people in recruitment, but these days your chances of meeting any of them are slim. Unless they are headhunters. The recruiters are there, but the internet has pushed them further away from the candidate experience. Their focus is now solely on their clients. As such, candidates need to seek ways to break the process, should they want better outcomes, and that means cutting out the middleman and connecting directly.

Candidate Experience

MOST candidate experiences are horrible.

At least LinkedIn provides an easy, streamlined way to present your CV and profile to the roles you wish to apply to. It gets wilder the minute you leave LinkedIn for external company applicant tracking systems (ATS). My personal discontent is with those applicant systems that require you spend a significant amount of time *manually* entering all the same information you have just uploaded, all for a role where you will have no feedback on your candidacy, and will in truth have a miniscule percentage chance of even speaking to an HR or hiring manager.

Many innovative companies demand these onerous, outdated approaches to identify candidates, but nothing is stored. Come back in a few months to apply to another interesting role, and you must start all over again. It shocks me how some of the world's largest firms can allow this horrific impression of themselves to be so publicly facing. One such company, a giant in my industry, I honestly stopped applying for, such was the catastrophe of their ATS and candidate experience.

> *Why do employers not put their talent acquisition through their own hiring processes? Employer brand is so important these days and horrific outward-facing ATS technology reflects directly on you, the employer!*

To those companies, and in fact any, I would urge their talent acquisition staff to do some blind applications through their own publicly facing systems and see how they like it, and I do mean going all the way to see just how much correspondence they receive on their applications. You must eat your own dog food, whether it be your product or any public interface to your company. It is as if the trial of applying is deliberately there to deter your interest. It is as if to say, "*You know what, we have already identified people for these roles, don't bother.*" Maybe this really is the truth of it! At the end of the day an internal referral will carry more weight than an external application, every time.

Companies need to focus on improving the candidate's experience in applying for jobs. Younger generations have grown up using well-designed apps with intuitive user interfaces like Snapchat and TikTok. These generations lead digital-first lives. If companies do not catch up to this, whole demographics of talent will pass them by. The payments industry has been hugely innovative in ensuring that ecommerce is a slick process, the last thing you want in a buying process is a payment engine you do not trust, or one that kicks you out of the site you are buying from. As such, a huge industry around "integrated payments" has grown up to support great customer experiences. Candidates, on the other hand, are treated like cattle, the industry around their recruitment correctly assuming that people will still continue to apply anyway. But if it is not built for the candidate, what can you expect? Let's face it, the candidate is the last priority as these systems were clearly designed and written for the benefit of the internal HR users only.

The Internet and Recruitment

The internet profoundly impacted our lives, disrupting countless business models, particularly in ecommerce, advertising, and media, where access to the mass market is key to success. Recruitment shares many similarities, connecting talent and employers through a powerful combination of advertising and direct communication, hence was itself ripe for disruption.

In the pre-internet era, recruiters held a monopoly on candidates, and the candidate experience was much more personal. You registered physically by visiting a high-street branch, you actually met a recruiter who would interview you. They represented you into companies they had on their books. It was a personalized experience. Recruiters served the candidate and the client equally. Given the catchment pool, hiring companies would happily work with a recruiter for their percentage fees on each successful placement. Recruitment processes were largely open, and a job advert would typically be an open call to receive relevant applications.

The internet blew all this up. Suddenly, the number of channels and the reach of online job postings grew exponentially. Hiring companies suddenly gained direct access to a world of talent. For candidates, choices also exploded. Consider what candidates can now access:

- Company Careers Websites.
- Social Networks: LinkedIn and/or Facebook.
- Jobs Boards: Monster, Indeed, eFinancial, and others.
- Recruiter Websites: Robert Walters, Hays, Randstad, and so on.
- Membership Websites: RegionUp, and so on.

The LinkedIn Effect

LinkedIn is a professional networking platform that connects professionals, companies, and recruiters globally. Launched in May 2003 with a mission to facilitate professional networking, career development, and recruitment, LinkedIn transformed the way companies find and attract talent. Most recruiters now depend on LinkedIn, the very platform that is both competing with them whilst being essential to their work. LinkedIn offers:

- **Professional Networking:** With over 1 billion members, LinkedIn has become the largest professional networking platform where 67 million companies are represented. Recruiters and hiring managers can leverage LinkedIn to identify and reach out to candidates with relevant skills and experience. This last point is key, now hiring managers and companies can create their own target candidate pools, and, if they have internal TAs, they can do away with working with outside recruitment agencies entirely. This was not possible prior to the advent of the internet and LinkedIn. From a networking point of view, 9,000 connections happen per minute. This is unparalleled.

  Sources—LinkedIn Sales Insights and LinkedIn internal data 2024.

- **Job Postings and Tools:** LinkedIn offers companies a platform to post job openings and to promote their employer brand to a global talent audience including specific recruitment tools, such as LinkedIn recruiter which allows for search and contact of passive candidates who might not be actively looking for moves at this time.

LinkedIn's key features include:

- **Profile Creation**: Members can create their personal digital profile, which essentially serves as an online résumé. Profiles include information on skills, work experiences, education, certification, endorsements, references, and professional accomplishments.
- **Networking:** LinkedIn allows for connection between members, whether they be classmates, colleagues, industry peers, or other professionals. Members can send connection requests, accept invitations, and send sales outreaches. They can also join interest or

knowledge based groups on subjects of interest or specialization. At no other time has networking been so trackable or usable.

- **Company Pages:** Companies can create profiles that showcase their brands, culture, achievements, and job openings. This creates a platform for sharing company updates and relevant content to engage with customers, employees, and talent pools.
- **Job Search and Recruitment:** LinkedIn features a job tool that allows users to search for job openings based on criteria such as location, industry, job title, and other key words.
- **LinkedIn Recruiter:** A tool for recruiting professionals to help streamline their recruitment processes. Offering enhanced search filtering, messaging, talent pool insights, including trends, integration with ATS, and more.
- **Groups and Communities:** Enabling users to join communities of professionals with shared interests, expertise, and industry specific discussions or affiliations. These groups provide platforms for discussions, networking, and knowledge sharing.
- **Content Publishing:** Users can publish posts, articles, and updates, to share insights, create a voice or platform for their product or services, and share expertise and learnings as well as thought leadership. This helps users establish and project their personal brand and drive engagement with users. If you are not already seeking to showcase your expertise and thought leadership to help elevate your status, then you should consider this.
- **Learning and Development:** A wide range of online course material, tutorials, and resources exist to help users develop new skills to advance their careers or stay up-to-date with industry trends.

Recruitment Up Close and Personal

What of the recruiters and the recruitment industry? We have touched on some of the changes, but these guys still exist, and the recruitment industry plays a significant role in the global economy. In terms of global market size, the recruitment industry is valued at approximately US$600 billion to US$700 billion annually. This includes contributions from staffing, recruitment process outsourcing (RPO), managed service providers (MSP), and executive search services.

External Recruiters

Here I am referring to generalist recruiters who work for one of the top four staffing or other focused recruitment agencies. These are not recruiters based within corporates but are serving corporates in the market. External recruitment is a highly managed sales function focusing only where efforts are most likely to receive reward. This is increasingly so as most companies will no longer offer exclusive recruitment rights for roles, unless highly specialized in nature, repeatable, or where a recruiter can offer access to an exclusive talent network. This lends itself well to roles such as compliance, accountancy, finance and software development, such as Java or full stack, backend or desktop. The point is that these roles are usually in high demand, therefore, a "Recruitment Desk" can profit and offer value to clients for a database of screened candidates who can plug into defined roles.

Often the recruiter in this case will be working with a "Sourcing Center," which will do the actual work of trawling LinkedIn for relevant profiles and performing initial outreach to qualify these candidates. This is a process known as "long listing," to create a "short list," of qualified candidates tested for their willingness to potentially move to another company or role. These shortlisted candidates are then presented to the recruiter who is managing the hiring company. The recruiter in this instance simply provides the profiles to the client for review and interview scheduling. Within this process, the recruiter does not engage with the candidate at all.

This means that regular repeatable jobs such as Java Engineers are more favored than so-called "Purple Squirrel" roles (a role that is so over specified, it describes the absolute perfect person in terms of attributes, skills, and experience, such that discovering the right candidate is like hunting for a needle in a haystack). Such roles are also less attractive to the generalized recruiter as they are generally one-off hires.

Simply in terms of expenditure of effort, focusing where there is volume makes sense. On average, a recruiter at a staffing agency like Randstad, Manpower, or Kelly might generate between US\$250,000 and

US$500,000 in booked revenue annually. This of course varies by region, sector, and so on and is highly impacted by general economic conditions, but the point remains. The battle between HR and the external recruiter over "who owns the candidate," if the same applicant pops up in both databases, is now a bane of the external recruiter's professional life. This neatly leads us onto the "Internal Recruiter" or "Talent Architect."

Talent Architects

These recruiters work directly in and for corporates. This person has probably come from one of the larger or specialist staffing firms, and these days they will mostly be working independently of agencies. Agencies are increasingly in competition with internal recruiters at companies, who have been set up to strive for direct marketplace or referred hiring, which is usually incentivized through staff bonuses for successful referral, (once the candidate passes their probationary period).

This is a direct product of widely available tools such as LinkedIn Recruiter becoming available in the market. It is also driven from an often-misguided idea that going direct is both cheaper and more efficient than using recruitment firms. As a result, hiring companies today are arguably less reliant on external recruiters. However, internal recruitment functions, unless outsourced, are typically part of a broader, generalist HR role that oversees all aspects of human resources within the business. This is an important distinction, internal HR teams are not specialized or fully dedicated to recruitment. In many cases, internal HR functions tend to be more transactional compared to external recruiters. While this is a general observation, it holds true for most organizations where HR teams manage recruitment alongside other responsibilities. This means they often lack the time, focus, or capacity to thoroughly screen and search for candidates as effectively as external recruiters can. Let's look at the various drivers as to why companies might not be using recruitment services so directly.

- **Cost Considerations:** The external recruitment model has traditionally been to charge a percentage fee of the candidate's annual salary. This could be as much as 15 to 25 percent or more, depending on the relationship, difficulty of hire, and the volume of hires. With an internal salaried TA working recruitment, the company will instead pay a commission to the referrer, which is lower than the market cost of using an outsourced agency or headhunter. The idea being that talent will come of its own accord, will be recommended, or found regardless. As such a 10 to 15 percent commission fee, for example, will be a cost-saving to the business.

- **Employer Brand Attraction:** Some companies feel that their reputation, the "desirability" of working for them, outweighs the need to work with external recruiters.
- **Control:** By handling recruitment directly, companies can tailor processes such as sourcing, interviewing, hiring decisions, and onboarding.
- **Access to Talent:** Social media, job boards, professional networking sites, and other tools have leveled the playing field significantly to a point whereby companies feel comfortable to take it all on themselves.
- **Expertise and Industry Knowledge:** Some companies may prefer to leverage their own industry expertise when screening and interviewing for candidates. Some industries may also enjoy closer networks than others.

The counterpoint to all of this is understanding how many open positions a TA team is handling. In this environment, the candidate is at a disadvantage. For these companies, it is crucial to have an internal advocate who can make a strong recommendation during the hiring process. Ultimately, this reinforces the need for candidates to adopt a networking approach. Relying solely on a generalist to fully grasp your skills, potential impact, and experience leaves too much to chance.

The Perfect Candidate

Increasingly in this digital and competitive world, there is a belief, or rather a demand, from hiring managers that candidates should perfectly "plug & play." Hiring managers and businesses are looking for candidates who can "hit the ground running," and deliver immediate business impact. There is no longer the luxury of bringing in a candidate who can be developed over time into their role, unless this role is a junior position where allowances will be made. That said, look at how many junior roles these days ask for relevant experience.

What does this mean in practice? It often leads to tighter hiring briefs, such as requests to specifically see candidates from their top five competitors. This narrow focus can overlook individuals with genuine potential, not only to perform the role, but also to excel, simply because they lack a particular company name on their CV, or because their industry-specific skills and experiences are misunderstood or missed altogether.

To succeed, candidates must find ways to stand out. This trend reinforces the importance of tapping into the connected job market and demonstrating the tangible impact they can make on business goals or key metrics. Essentially, candidates need to adopt a "business case" or ROI mindset when presenting themselves, showing the clear value their hire would bring.

AI

We have spoken a great deal about the failure of the candidate experience in modern-day recruitment. Artificial Intelligence (AI) is poised to significantly transform the recruitment industry, offering numerous advantages while also introducing new challenges.

The promise of AI lies in its ability to transform the candidate experience by making the process faster, fairer, and more personalized. AI can streamline administrative tasks, such as résumé screening, freeing up recruiters to focus on meaningful human interactions once more. Advanced algorithms can reduce unconscious bias by evaluating candidates solely on skills and qualifications, fostering greater inclusivity. Furthermore, AI could deliver personalized feedback, improve matching between candidates and roles, and provide insights into career growth opportunities, creating a more engaging and satisfying journey for applicants.

This is the promise. The reality at least at the moment seems a little bleaker for candidates. The statistic that 75 percent of résumés are rejected by an ATS before reaching a human has been widely cited in recruitment studies and articles. ATS filter applications based on specific criteria such as keywords, formatting, and job relevance. Formatting of presented formats can also be a real issue, with the ATS not recognizing layouts, images, or document types. The lesson is not to use fancy or image-laden CV formats.

Source: CNBC.com Kerri Anne Renzulli Article published February 28, 2019.

While AI may potentially help the recruitment industry focus more on the candidate and human experience, it will not help ensure you are the one in prime position to be hired. Do not wait for the AI revolution. Ensure that you focus your activities where you will gain the maximum outcomes.

Candidate Frustrations

The internet opened every organizational role to a global audience. Hence, the sheer volume of candidate applications for any role often means that résumés may never be seen by a human initially, as automated systems filter them out based on specific keywords. Any recruiter will also not be looking in fine detail, they want to grasp the essence of your application and your experience to quickly qualify you in or out for the next phase of screening. As mentioned, this could literally come down to which companies the hiring manager wants to see candidates from. Many mainstream bulk recruiters operate this way also, whereby they explicitly ask the hiring manager where they would like to see CVs from. This can make the process feel impersonal and arbitrary. I have often found myself eminently qualified for published roles, but rejected on the basis that the companies I had worked for were not recognized by the hiring process. Sourcing center search processes are also only as good as the keywords utilized to long and short-list potential candidates.

> *Do not spend a lot of time customizing your CV for each application you make. It is not worth it. You are better off focusing on your keywords and simplifying your CV to a handful of versions you will use for different types of roles. Unless you are working with confidential search or headhunters, no one is going to be studying your CV in detail. It's a sad truth.*

When applying through a job board, or re-entering your details ad nauseam on a third-party candidate ATS, it can feel as if you are simply throwing Hail Marys with very small chances of being noticed or processed through to the next stage of the application or interview process. The lack of personalized communication or feedback then leaves candidates uncertain about their application status and what they could improve. Without feedback, many candidates will blindly continue their application approaches without any modification, as they simply do not know what is working and what is not.

Others may attempt to build their CV and candidacy letters with the advertised role in mind, but again this is time-consuming and, if no feedback is coming, ultimately not worth it. I go back to my connected job market interview story. The bank in that instance was hiring from the same cloth because organizationally they take candidates from other banks or from one of the payment schemes. They will not be looking for companies they do not so readily recognize where your actual experience might have been honed on topics or skills applicable for the role. They will discard your application as opposed to trying to understand it and why you are potentially more qualified. They will certainly not be calling you to discuss your application. It is a systematic weakness in the industry. That is why you have to bypass the HR and TA all together to make your case directly.

Poorly written or unclear job descriptions can make it challenging for candidates to determine if they are a good fit for the role as well. Lack of clarity can lead candidates to fill in the blanks or question whether they are uniquely qualified or wasting their time. It is better with these applications to not expect an acknowledgment of your application, unless it is machine-generated. Do not expect a recruiter or HR representative to reach out, expect in rare cases, and do not expect any feedback in relation to your application or if the position has closed. By all means keep these applications in your repertoire, (if you cannot identify the hiring manger and go direct), but do not place any emotional investment into them. Fire them off and hope for the best. Consider them shots in the dark, mostly they are no better than that. If you do get a callback to interview, count your luck, the roulette wheel has spun favorably towards you.

Focus on Networking

There is a problem, but it is unfair to blame the industry. Recruiters are hardworking folks in a pressurized industry with many competitors, including the very companies whose jobs they represent. Exceptions exist, headhunters take the time to truly understand the candidates they represent, typically for senior-level roles. Additionally, some recruiters focus on confidential placements with a degree of exclusivity, offering a more personalized approach. However, these opportunities come rarely and are usually reserved for top-tier hires. So, if you encounter a recruiter, be kind. Understanding the system you're navigating helps you respond more effectively.

The question is, would you rather go through a generalist, or speak directly to the hiring manager who has more expertise in your role, and who would be better able to interpret your fit to all the relevant criteria? Better to get their attention so that your application might be highlighted and then come through the usual HR process. The key to success is to ensure that you are in the conversation in the first place.

Many job opportunities, particularly high-value roles, are never publicly advertised and, instead, emerge through conversations, referrals, and professional connections. Networking allows candidates to showcase their personality, adaptability, and values in a way that no algorithm can interpret. Employers often prioritize candidates recommended by trusted colleagues or contacts, as these referrals come with an implicit endorsement of credibility and fit. Keep networking and keep differentiating, focus on the connected job market, and you will succeed more, gain better results, and impact your life and career more fruitfully.

Starting to Stand Out Against Your Competition

Look at company sales presentations. Ask the top four companies in any industry to come and present to you. I would put money on the fact that you will see four very similar presentations, talking about *their* companies, *their* services and scope, *their* credentials and experience, all within *their* own specific corporate language. They will all claim market dominance and be able to claim large, recognized clients. You will have to decipher what their products and services mean within your own environment. Simply talking about things that interest you whilst demonstrating no curiosity or initiative about the audience is the mark of a terrible interaction. Be better than this as a candidate.

Differentiation allows you to rise above the majority. Few candidates will tailor their interview to the hiring company based upon prior research. As such, they will all begin to look quite similar. The interviewer has now to work harder to assess who stands out in terms of potential impact, values, behaviors, and applied experience for the role. One after another they will see the same things, CVs that detail no accomplishments and passive, underprepared candidates with no stories to illustrate how they would fit into and contribute to the role on offer.

You will only have a handful of opportunities to lift your profile and yourself above the crowd. You must be able to recognize, seize, and deliver in these moments. Remember, this is no guarantee of success, but, if you do, you will raise your chances, I promise you.

Takeaways

- *All roads lead to the connected job market if you really want a chance to carve out better opportunities for yourself.*
- *Do not get lost in the crowd of lazy applications.*
- *Find your internal champions to support your candidacy and prioritize it through to the HR and TA representatives. Only then formally apply.*
- *Respond to the what the hiring managers are demanding, show your worth in your direct conversation with them, demonstrate the approaches and outputs you would focus on and with what returns based upon your experience, values, behaviors, and philosophies, all tied to their corporate language and priorities, as you have researched and understood them to be.*

CHAPTER 3

The Need to Differentiate

Chapter Summary

- Still not convinced about the connect job market? Potentially fear and inertia are playing a role.
- Differentiate now!
- You…only better. Think about adopting a sales approach to your candidacy.
- How to be more outcome-oriented and how to produce ROI-driven applications.

In today's competitive job market, blending in is a fast track to being overlooked. To stand out, candidates must master the art of differentiation, showcasing what sets them apart isn't just an option, it's the key to unlocking career success.

Why Is Change So Hard?

Change is hard because we are often dealing with deeply ingrained habits and behaviors that have created neural pathways in our brains making it uncomfortable to adopt new behaviors. We are wired to follow the path of least resistance, which is typically the one we have created through our past thoughts and actions. When we try to change, we are going to be fighting against these tendencies, which requires energy and focus. Additionally, we tend to rationalize our current behaviors, especially if they have served us well in the past. Change is not just about deciding to do things differently. It requires consistent effort and is a process, not an overnight event. Resistance to change is a natural part of being human, but recognizing and working through it is essential for personal and professional growth. In respect to recruitment, many of us are simply engrained with ideas about how the process should work. We are less receptive to the realities of our experience. It's easy to complain about the fact that the candidate experience is broken, far less easy to do something radically different, and especially if that approach forces us outside of our comfort zone.

Differentiation

Hopefully, you are seeing reasons for acting more directly within the connected job market. If you are still wavering, let's look at the issue from the recruiter's perspective. They are swamped. Exact figures are difficult to pinpoint, as they vary by industry, job type, and platform, but it's common to see hundreds of applicants for a single job posting. Typically, only about 10 percent of those applicants make it to the interview stage.

- **Response by Platform:**
  - **Job Boards:** These tend to generate a high volume of applicants, often 200 to 300 per job post. However, many of these applicants may not be well qualified, or may well live abroad, leading to more screening time for employers.
  - **Company Websites:** Job postings on a company's career page generally receive about 50 to 100 applicants on average, often from candidates who are specifically interested in that company, that said, many will also be applying on an aspirational basis.
  - **LinkedIn Job Posts:** LinkedIn reports that job listings on its platform receive an average of 120 applicants per post, though these numbers vary based on the visibility of the advert.

Application quality is a real issue. Factoring in sheer volume, understandably the review process will favor quick whittling down of the stack to focus on the few CVs that will be advanced. Unsuitable applications will be discarded based on unfavorable geographies, (companies will not consider relocation costs outside of the most senior positions), those without experience, and those who do not fit the profile based on companies they have worked in. So, yes, the candidate process is broken, but the recruiters are also up against it. If at stage one your application is not immediately standing out, then you will be discarded.

How to Differentiate?

A CV is not a person, and people are not hiring CVs.

To improve your chances of standing out, you must start thinking in terms of differentiation. By conducting targeted research and identifying what truly drives you, you can craft compelling stories for interviews that will shape how you present yourself moving forward. Achieving this requires a shift of mindset toward how you think and speak about yourself. For many, this will involve a need to overcome a natural reticence toward self-promotion. It is true that many people are uncomfortable with the idea of selling themselves. This can be due to long-held stereotypical notions that sales is somehow sleazy or that self-promotion might be seen to be boastful. So, let's begin by defining what sales really is.

Sales

Sales is about solving for a particular set of issues, which in turn requires the salesperson to be able to spot and define a value proposition. This requires active listening and an ability to ask great questions. Only then can the seller speak the other person's language, as opposed to their own. A value proposition is demonstrating what your solution is going to provide and what the outcome will be, in value, cost-savings, or opportunity terms. This is basically what an interview is about. Your role as the candidate is to uncover:

- What are the organizational focuses and goals?
- What are the challenges?
- What impact can you make?
- What might be the opportunity cost of not selecting you?
- How do your values and behaviors fit the organizational culture, and how can you serve and extend this?

In interviewing the hiring company, you must uncover what these vital clues are, which will then allow you to speak to how you are going to solve for their issues. This requires you to clearly communicate your values and philosophies, demonstrating how you will address challenges through the focus, skills, and the experience you bring to the table. This again is basic sales.

Think of interview as a consultative process of proving why you are the best choice for the role, through the examples and stories you tell about your experiences and achievements. In delivering this well, you are going to start to form a close partnership and expertise in knowing the hiring company, and the hiring manager, for whom you are going to deliver the value that you have identified.

If you are one of those people who is concerned, nervous, or reticent about putting yourself in the shop window, ask yourself whether the process described above is different to your perception. Sales is really not about being aggressive, boastful, or unaligned to your audience's needs and ambitions.

We will look at this whole topic in greater detail in Chapter 9: Everyone Should Be a Salesperson. Find your Sales Philosophy. If you are reserved on this topic, you need to contextualize your fear, which can lead to inactivity, and engage a sense of what you must do to succeed in achieving what you desire and deserve. Believe you me, I can tell you something about nervousness. I have spent a career in an industry where many, including myself, would have initially identified as introverts. It's not an unusual sensation, when you are called to give public presentations, speeches, and key notes. The fear of being thrust outside your comfort zone is very real indeed, but this is also the space within which you will find your greatest opportunities for growth. In writing books and posting online, I can also tell you something about that nervousness when you hover over the post button wondering how your message will land. All of this is a natural response to instincts that have been hardwired into our brains over millennia. Fear of failure, fear of going it alone instead of together in a group, and fear of humiliation and ridicule.

My advice is always to put things into a more positive perspective. I can tell you that folks are in the majority supportive of anyone trying to put value into the world. You would, for example, be amazed and gratified by the support provided by your network should you turn to them in a time of need, provided of course that you do so in an honest, authentic manner that is not badgering or insensitive to someone's time and focus.

Also consider this. I have been the interviewer many times, and nothing is worse, more time-wasting, than meeting someone who has booked an interview, only to come to have you lead a conversation off their CV. Because now the interviewer must do all the work to discern whether this person can bring you any value to the role or organization. Counter to this, any interviewer would welcome someone well prepared, someone who has done their research, someone who has had the courage to come with a perspective as to how they would take the role, their perceptions about the business, its values and targets to the next level, irrespective of role or function.

Anyone doing this will demonstrate their cultural fit in action. You cannot do that as a passive candidate. To be proactive, to take control, shows initiative. It demonstrates courage, and it almost guarantees that you will receive feedback, as well as coaching for the next steps. Those who receive no feedback during or post-interview most likely have given nothing of themselves in the process, hence, there is nothing to give back to them. Any interviewer is hoping for a great two-way conversation with a candidate.

What Is Your ROI?

Candidates need to shift toward a return on investment (ROI) approach to their candidacy.

Many a time, I have taken a stalled interview process through to contract by switching to a focus on the ROI that I would provide in the proposed role. This is achieved by showcasing measurable achievements, emphasizing how contributions have driven results in previous roles. Focusing on ROI during an interview can be highly beneficial for a candidate for several reasons:

- **Shows Business Acumen:** An ROI mentality demonstrates a clear understanding of how businesses operates and makes money, highlighting your leadership potential where decision-making impacts the bottom line.

- **Highlights Impact:** Through highlighting how your skills, experience, and work ethic can transform the organization, focusing not just on past achievements but also on how you can deliver tangible benefits for your potential employer.
- **Differentiation:** Many candidates can list skills and experiences, but those who can connect these to business outcomes really stand out by demonstrating contribution to the larger goals of the organization.
- **Aligns with Organizational Goals:** ROI aligns yourself with organizational goals and shows that you are results-oriented and focused on contributing to success.
- **Prepares for Leadership:** ROI approaches show that you are ready to take on responsibilities that involve managing resources effectively through making decisions that will benefit the organization financially.

The key to a successful interview is not just showcasing your skills but showing how you will help the organization succeed. Here are some steps to help you identify where you can highlight your potential impact:

- **Quantify Success**: Include specific metrics from your past, such as revenue growth, cost savings, productivity improvements, or customer satisfaction scores, to illustrate tangible value. Example: "*I increased sales by 25% over six months, generating an additional US$200K in revenue. I did this through…*[define behaviors, philosophy, and approach]."
- **Problem-Solving Impact**: Describe how you identified challenges, implemented solutions, and delivered measurable outcomes that benefited the organization. Example: "*I redesigned a workflow that reduced project turnaround time by 30%, enabling a faster time-to-market. The key to this was…*[define the outcomes delivered]."
- **Align with Employer Goals**: Tailor your application to demonstrate how your skills and experience will directly support the company's priorities, like boosting profitability, market share, or operational efficiency. Example: "*I am expert in streamlining*

recruitment pipelines, having cut hiring costs by 20% while main-taining top-tier talent quality. My philosophy on this is…[define approach], *I specifically took the following actions…*[define actions], *which led to…*[define outcomes]."

By focusing on concrete value and aligning it with the employer's objectives, candidates can stand out as ROI-driven professionals. Chapter 13: Shaping the Interview Process and Post-Interview Strategies, looks at how you can encapsulate your ROI into a one-pager that can be used post-interview and within second or third interviews, to shape the conversation toward your proposed approaches and focused outcomes in role. These are the tools that in my experience immediately convert interviews into job offers.

Takeaways

- *Think about a sales-led approach to your candidacy and understand the positive impact such an approach can bring, combined with your networking and research activities.*
- *Think about how you have delivered outcomes in the past, and what those were.*
- *If you are taking a step-up, consider what you have learned from others on your journey and how you would take those experiences to drive outcomes in the role you are going for.*

CHAPTER 4

Headhunters and Confidential Hire

> ## Chapter Summary
>
> - Not all recruiters are the same, understand how to get their attention.
> - Headhunter or confidential hire processes are desirable, connect to key recruitment players in your industry.

Other Recruiters

The thesis so far may have the impression of being quite anti-recruitment. Certainly, I am mostly disappointed with the recruitment experience. You should be aware that I have a wide network of contacts in the industry globally, and honestly, many of them would share my perspective.

What cannot be denied is the fact that these folks are sincere, passionate, and came into the recruitment industry with high principles and philosophies of helping industries and individuals to find each other. With that in mind, I want to emphasize that I write primarily from the candidate's perspective. Most would agree that the candidate experience is subpar. However, despite the challenges we have addressed, there is still a part of the recruitment industry that operates differently. I'm referring to headhunters and those who specialize in "confidential hire."

Headhunters and Confidential Hire Recruiters

It's all beginning to sound like Game of Thrones with all the talk of heads and confidential approaches, isn't it? Let's take a moment to understand these types of recruiters and why they are different and also, crucially, how you can attract their interest.

Typically, these recruiters will be operating out of what might be called "boutique" firms. By their very nature, they are likely not focusing on high-turnover, high-volume placement work. Instead, these firms will be working on a regional, even global basis, and seeking to place high-level to senior roles, even highly specialized or technical ones, but in all cases, roles of a strategic nature, whereby the placement of the right candidate is the most important criteria.

As candidates, we must be conscious of how these recruiters find us, and this is where keywords within our LinkedIn profiles are super important. LinkedIn searches, Boolean strings, and sourcing centers might be at play, so please attend to the suggestions within this book about ensuring that your LinkedIn profile is optimized, so that you might be discovered. For more practical advice on optimizing your LinkedIn profile refer to Chapter 6: LinkedIn and Building a Powerful Presence. Here are the most critical elements:

Keyword Optimization for Search Engine Optimization (SEO)

- **Your LinkedIn Headline**: This should go beyond your job title. Use keywords that headhunters might search for, such as "Executive Leadership," "Operations Management," or "Strategy Expert," along with your industry or role specialties.
- **Skills and Endorsements**: Add relevant skills to your profile that reflect your expertise and industry. This helps in making your profile more searchable. Ensure that you collect endorsements and references focused on your previous roles and expertise also.
- **Job Titles and Experience**: Ensure your past roles reflect the terminology recruiters use. Use standard job titles that are recognizable in your industry. Do not use acronyms or overly technical or internalized language. Do outline your focuses, initiatives, achievements, and learnings within these sections in concise bullet-point formats.
- **Summary (About Section)**: Write a strong, clear summary, incorporating keywords related to your career goals, skills, industry, experience, and achievements. Mention that you are open to confidential opportunities, if appropriate.

Industry-Specific Focus

- **Industry Selection**: Make sure that you have chosen the correct industry in your profile. Recruiters often filter by industry, so this is crucial to ensure you are in their search results.
- **Targeted Content**: Share and engage with content relevant to your industry or field of expertise. This can position you as a thought leader or subject-matter expert, increasing your visibility to recruiters. It is important to create a professional voice within your network.

Use the "Open to Work" Feature (Confidentially)

LinkedIn allows you to signal to recruiters that you are open to new opportunities without publicly displaying this to your network. Customize this option so that only recruiters can see it. This boosts your chances of being discovered for confidential or discreet roles.

- **Confidentiality Notes**: Subtly mention that you're open to confidential or executive searches in your summary or under your "open to work" settings.
- **Use Discreet Language**: Phrasing like "Open to confidential executive opportunities" signals that you may be available without being explicit, if you are currently employed.

Network with Recruiters and Headhunters

A good way to get onto the radar of executive and confidential hire recruiters is to actively participate in their networks online. A lot of this will happen organically if you are active on LinkedIn, but it pays to have a proactive approach to this as well.

- **Profile Completeness**: Make sure your profile is 100 percent complete, signaling to headhunters that you are serious about your professional presence.
- **Regular Updates**: Keep your profile updated with new accomplishments, certifications, and experiences.

- **Connections**: Build a network of recruiters, especially those specializing in confidential hiring or executive search in your industry. Connecting with them increases the likelihood of being noticed. Try to build these connections face to face. This can help in regard to receiving feedback and ideas, as well as hearing about opportunities you would be well-suited for. Having coffee with a well-connected, informed recruiter can tell you a lot about the state of the marketplace, about which firms and industries are hiring, and about what opportunities these folks are currently prioritizing.
- **Engagement**: Engage with posts from recruiters or headhunters. This raises your visibility and keeps your profile active. Consider this as part of your overall posting strategy.

Achievements

Ensure that you highlight your achievements in clear outcome-based details on your professional profile. If you are struggling to bring this to life, start with the challenge, detail the approaches, and show your results in quantifiable terms.

- **Quantifiable Results**: Recruiters love to see concrete numbers and results. Highlight your achievements in role, particularly those that show leadership, strategic influence, or high-level decision-making (e.g., "Increased revenue by 20%" or "Led a team of 50 professionals" or "Turned around a nonperforming team to double revenue in under two years.")
- **Leadership Experience**: If you're targeting high-level or executive roles, ensure your profile reflects leadership skills, project management, and decision-making experience. Ensure that you are speaking in terms of the mission, the horizons, the focuses, and outputs you have attained.

Recommendations

Do not neglect recommendations and endorsements on your LinkedIn profile. These lend credibility and can serve as your set of references. If you are starting from scratch, reach out to previous managers and leaders, or to well-positioned colleagues who you feel might offer you a written endorsement. In some cases, folks will ask you to draft a paragraph for them. Make sure the endorsement you create is accurate and speaks to your personal and professional attributes and approaches, including outcomes or achievements. Finally, whenever you move role or company, ensure that your profile is up-to-date and is relevant.

- **Strong Endorsements**: Request recommendations from colleagues or clients who can vouch for your qualities and results. Headhunters often pay attention to this as an indicator of your reputation and capabilities.
- **"Recommendations" on LinkedIn**: You have to search for this on your profile. It is below the "Skills" tab (Figure 4.1).

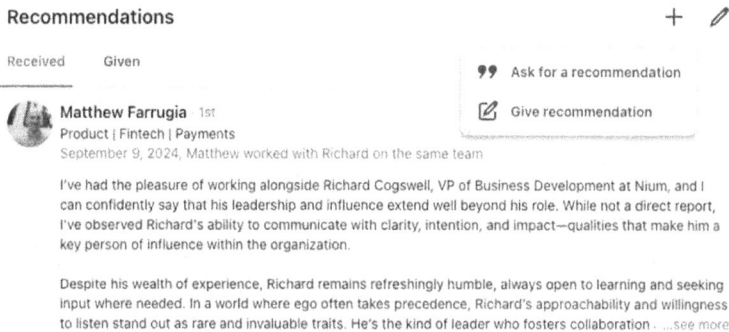

Figure 4.1 LinkedIn recommendations example

From here, click on the "+" symbol to be prompted to "ask for a recommendation" or to "give a recommendation." Always, offer to reciprocate, or even proactively provide recommendations for others as part of asking for them in return.

How Confidential Hire and Headhunters Work

Once they have identified you, an outreach email, or a LinkedIn InMail offering a screening conversation is made. This first conversation is where the opportunity is explained, and your interest is ascertained. Some other elements such as your experience and your commercial necessities may also be covered, such as your package requirements, notice period, and so on. These recruiters will usually want to meet you face to face, geography allowing, and will want to spend time with you to better understand your background, skills, experiences, and motivations. They will not only want to demonstrate a powerful candidate pool to the hiring company, but will also want to represent you to their fullest capacity. They will also coach you in terms of who you will be meeting, their focuses, style of leadership, and so on. You can also bounce ideas off them and dig deep on issues or challenges that the company or hiring manager may be facing.

Expect to be well briefed for your interviews and be prepared to ask detailed questions about the company, the hiring manager, and their goals and motivations. What makes the headhunters of this world stand out is their desire for you to win. They will fight hard for you and will ensure that you have all the information you need in order to also represent them well.

The experience will be everything that we have expected of the industry and which has been snuffed out over time with the internet, technology, and changing talent acquisition practices. The downside? These recruiters and opportunities are few and far in number. The quality is high, and the processes pleasurable. You will be competing with the best in terms of other candidates, thus, you cannot bank on winning these roles every time. What will be different within this process is that, should you not be successful, you will know someone qualified did win through in the end. You will also learn from the experience as feedback will be provided at all turns.

The moral of this story is to make sure you are easily and correctly identified as a potential candidate by this type of recruiter. The rest is again up to you, in terms of how well you promote and represent yourself. What you will not have to do with these approaches is work so hard to get in front of the hiring panel. Do consider use of the approaches covered in Chapter 13: Shaping the Interview Process and Post-Interview Strategies, but focus that effort on essentially showing your qualities over and above the other talented candidates the headhunter will have assembled for the hiring panel to consider.

Takeaways

- *Network with headhunters and confidential hire recruiters.*
- *Ensure that your LinkedIn profile sells you well and is set up for identifying you for the roles you want.*
- *Ensure that you are using your "Recommendations" functionality in an optimal fashion.*
- *Do your own preparation and research prior to interview and ensure that you leverage the insights available from the headhunter. Ensure you focus on the company and hiring manager's focuses, culture, leadership style, challenges, and expected outcomes of the role and ask "what does success look like within a year for the winning candidate?"*
- *Do not put all your money down, along with all your hopes and dreams on a confidential hire opportunity, be of the mindset that it is an opportunity to be taken seriously, be thankful for it, but know you will be competing with an "enhanced" field of candidates.*

CHAPTER 5

Being Out of Work

Chapter Summary

- Being out of work can be one of the most challenging experiences anyone can have, it requires self-reflection, good planning, self-management, resilience, and the courage to get out there with a positive forward-thinking mindset.
- The average time for a senior exec to be rehired can be anything up to 6 months. Be prepared for that timeline to extend even further than you might be comfortable with.
- Time is something you will need to manage positively.
- Consider your financial position and make budget decisions early.
- Focus on hobbies, mental well-being, physical fitness, and family during this challenging time.
- Use your network, in creative ways. Be visible, focus on your outreach, and don't just rely on existing connections. Follow-up diligently.
- Stay positive and use any opportunities you can to stay "match fit" for interview.

Redundancy

A great defense, should the unexpected come, is to have an active and growing network to which you are regularly contributing. Do not wait until your need is greatest. Build, nurture, and be a good servant to your network now, especially when you do not need it.

Throughout the course of your career, the likelihood of being out of work is a very real prospect. Even if you are stable and performing in a role, you can never be complacent. An acquisition, a merger, an economic or sector downturn, a pandemic, any of these situations could see you unexpectedly on the job market having been made redundant.

This can be an especially challenging time, especially in the face of monetary and life commitments and especially so if you are a senior executive. If you are under monetary pressure, everything can be heightened, because not only is this seemingly all about you, but being jobless comes with a stack of other concerns and emotions. Much of this will depend on your personal circumstances and family situation, of course. You may be lucky, but the chances are that if you are not currently and sufficiently active within your network, you might find yourself looking for work from a standing start, which is hardly ideal.

Much will have changed for you. You may be feeling a range of emotions, and many of them could be negative. You might even be in mourning and possibly in a state of disbelief, especially if you defined yourself through the company, role, position, team, or the culture you have left behind. Losing a role that was not just a job, but a significant part of your identity can feel like losing a part of yourself. The bonds formed with colleagues and the shared commitment to the company's goals can make the separation feel personal and painful. This emotional upheaval can lead to a period of grief and uncertainty, affecting both personal and professional aspects of life as you navigate this transition. As hard as it might be, now is the time to let go of this lightly, to sharpen the experiences and stories you can take forward toward the only focus you need to have now, the work of finding yourself a new opportunity.

Time

You will have to find ways to be comfortable with time, because you will now have more than you are perhaps used to. Free from deadlines and assignments, meetings, and the focuses of corporate life, you will now have to make your own schedule and plan accordingly to succeed in finding your next opportunity. Time is not respected by the job market. Hiring is a process that can take a very long time, even if you are networking your way into a role, as the role has to be defined, approved, budgeted, and opened up to other candidates well before you can think to receive a formal offer and start date. You will also have to learn to manage yourself and your emotional state in a way you may not be used to doing. Ensuring that you see yourself as a vital part of the journey you are about to undertake is essential to making a success of the venture. Consider this early and protect your mental and physical health throughout the process. Consider your financial position and prepare to budget early on if needed.

Negative Emotions

Focus on any emotions you are feeling and do not suppress these, especially negative ones, they are natural and normal. We will discuss emotions more in Chapter 10: Fear and Inertia, specifically in the context of learning how to recognize and manage these in the process of networking to develop your own opportunities.

What I have learned through the course of my career is that emotions should not be suppressed in anyway. Equally importantly, it is not good enough to merely acknowledge them and move on without unpacking them. Learning to listen to yourself and understanding what you are feeling is as important a data set in the context of anything you are trying to achieve as any other. Take this moment to seek to understand what you are feeling and recast anything negative into a more positive mindset. Not only will this help you show up as best as you can in your endeavors, but it can also help ensure you are not putting obstacles in the path to creating and then maximizing the opportunities for hire ahead of you.

Time to Hire

There could be a direct correlation between your experience, seniority, and the time it takes to secure your next gig. This on the face of it seems very hard to take. One might assume the opposite, that hard earned experience and skills might be highly sought after in any job market or economy. However, the opposite is often the case. More years in work equals more months potentially unemployed. On average, it can take senior managers or leaders around 6 to 12 months to find a new job, reflecting the complexity and selectiveness of the hiring process.

The other factor is that you can never predict the state of the economy or hiring cycles at the point you are let go. Even now, post-pandemic, there are many sectors hesitating when it comes to hiring. You might even find that you are being labeled suddenly as "overqualified" for roles. This can be a blow especially if there is financial pressure on you, or if you are genuinely looking to redress work-life balance. How many times are senior-level candidates told, for example, *"this role is too junior for you?"* Unfortunately, given the transactional nature of most recruitment these days, you are more likely to get a boilerplate rejection such as this, rather than someone taking the time to reach out and understand your goals, motivations, and drivers for taking a so-called "smaller role."

The reasons for this are varied. The job market for senior positions is narrower, with fewer vacancies compared to entry or midlevel roles. This scarcity means greater competition among highly qualified candidates. Additionally, organizations seeking senior leaders often have rigorous hiring processes, including multiple interview rounds and assessments, which extend the time required to secure a position. This assumes the role is approved, budgeted for, and that there are no other blockers that could affect the timing of the process, such as wider senior-level redundancies or cost-cutting measures happening in the firm. All the stars need alignment in this regard.

If you do find yourself suddenly in this unfortunate position, it is far better to prepare yourself early for a campaign, and a longer one than you might hope for. Consider the possibility of being out of work for an extended period and plan your time and resources accordingly. Campaigns take stamina and will for them to succeed. Think about taking a holistic approach early on, which frames your goal and mission alongside other factors, such as managing yourself, keeping active, and maintaining physical and mental health (Figure 5.1).

Quick Wins

While we prepare for a drawn-out saga, we of course must put our best efforts into resolving the situation fast. My last redundancy came in the first quarter of 2021, soon after the pandemic restrictions were being lifted, hardly a good time for hiring within my industry as most companies in my space had been cutting back their operations to ride out this unprecedented period of reduced business flow. I had 3 months before I would be missing my salary.

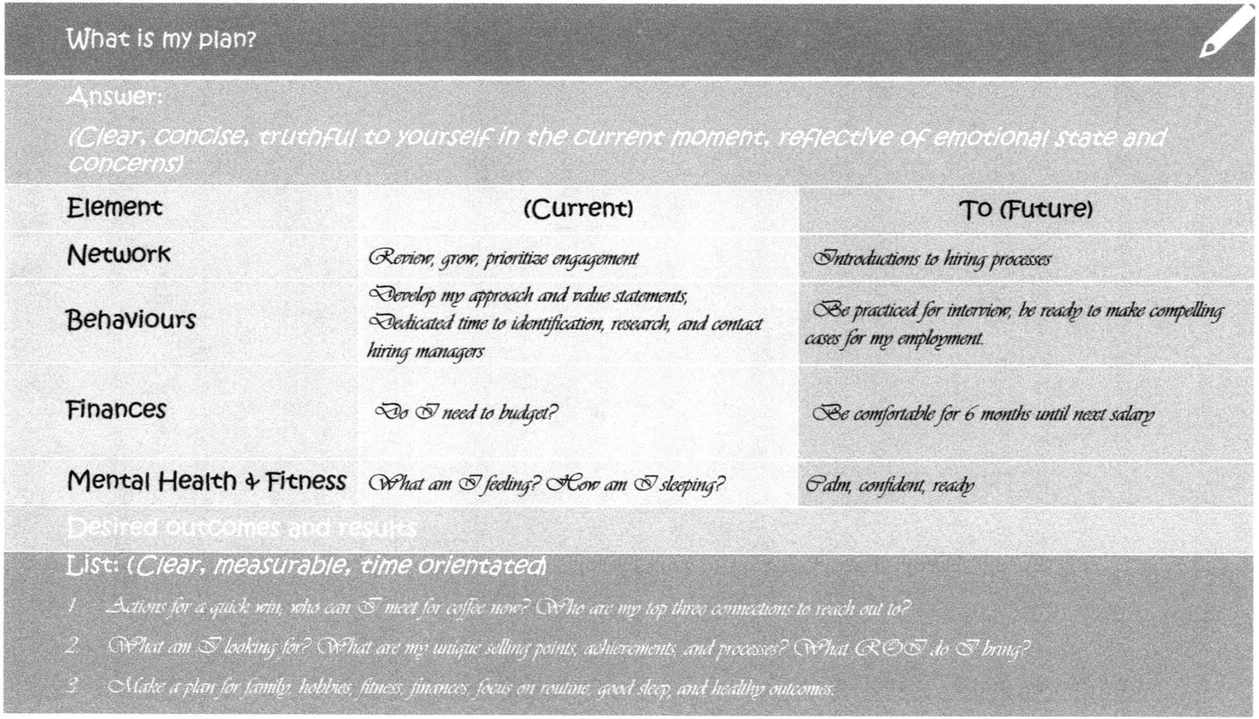

What is my plan?		
Answer:		
(Clear, concise, truthful to yourself in the current moment, reflective of emotional state and concerns)		
Element	**(Current)**	**To (Future)**
Network	Review, grow, prioritise engagement	Introductions to hiring processes
Behaviours	Develop my approach and value statements; Dedicated time to identification, research, and contact hiring managers	Be practiced for interview, be ready to make compelling cases for my employment
Finances	Do I need to budget?	Be comfortable for 6 months until next salary
Mental Health & Fitness	What am I feeling? How am I sleeping?	Calm, confident, ready
Desired outcomes and results		
List: (Clear, measurable, time orientated)		

1 Actions for a quick win, who can I meet for coffee now? Who are my top three connections to reach out to?

2 What am I looking for? What are my unique selling points, achievements, and processes? What ROI do I bring?

3 Make a plan for family, hobbies, fitness, finances, focus on routine, good sleep, and healthy outcomes

Figure 5.1 Considerations for those out of work

Thankfully, this was also a time when we were able to freely move about and meet one another face to face. I immediately looked to my network and set up two coffee meetings, both with senior leaders who were well-connected within my industry. This is an important exercise to quickly undertake. Think who within your network is the best connected and most likely to be able to introduce you to either opportunities or to other folks who might be able to aid in some way.

Being honest and transparent is the best approach in these circumstances. There is no shame in being in this position. Mine was triggered by an acquisition, which due to the COVID pandemic had become an environment whereby the acquired, not the acquirer, was now in charge of leading the consolidation of our business divisions as the buying price had been substantially cut due to the pandemic. So, when the conversation had moved on from the usual pleasantries of meeting a partner in the industry and to the question of how the merger of the two businesses was going, I was able to lay the scenario out on the table.

The first coffee catch-up was a terrific boost for my morale, as the understanding and support I received was so generous. It was also a rich source of introductions to people who are now a vibrant part of my network. It was the second meeting that started the ball rolling and led to my next role, which I managed to secure within a month. It was still an interview process I had to take control of, but it did lead to a contract, and I will show you how I did that in later chapters.

The morale of the story is to strike fast, set up meetings, and be active and present in trying to get to introductory conversations about your future employment. Do this while you are planning your overall strategy and approaches. You never know what will come. Take the meetings, have a sense of what you want, and accept the graciousness and generosity of others, whether it be an introduction to another contact or something more palpable. If you can hit gold quickly, thank those who helped, be gracious to yourself for making it happen, and count your blessing with gratitude.

The Darker Moments of an Extended Job Search

I have had four experiences of redundancy. On two occasions, I have been able to find my next role almost immediately. In fact, on one occasion

I managed this within the same day. I achieved this by utilizing my network effectively, and I was lucky enough to be introduced on both occasions to people looking to hire to my profile.

Twice I suffered prolonged and painful periods out of work as I tried, in a suppressed hiring environment, to find my next role. Once I was out of work for the best part of a year. I had to focus on maintaining a healthy, positive mindset and to systematically find my next gig. This was an incredibly tough time. This is why I suggest it is best to steel yourself for a harder journey, while taking actions to potentially and hopefully make it much easier.

> *Planning is bringing the future into the present so that you can do something about it now.*
>
> Attributed to Alan Lakein

Recognize Your Starting Point

Take a moment to acknowledge how you are feeling. Putting this down on paper is a good place to start to acknowledge where you are at. Beginning to put down a plan is also about being able to manage the roller-coaster of emotions you are more than likely to be feeling as you embark on this journey. Be watchful for the following;

- Loss of sleep.
- Moments of joy and hope.
- Moments of pure fear and depression.
- Anger and frustration.
- Loneliness.
- Disillusionment.
- Stress.
- Imposed or desired social isolation.
- Shame or embarrassment.

Sustained motivation can be tough. A plan will hold you together and give you focus, especially when progress is slow and times are difficult.

Talk to Friends and Family

This is an important step toward not suppressing emotions and to ensure that you do not carry the burdens alone. Do consider this early, as I know, for some, the temptation is not to want to discuss the situation with anyone, it's already hard enough to process yourself.

You may be feeling a sense of shame or failure, but you will receive so much valuable support from those who know and love you. Also, it will prevent difficult social or emotional problems later down the track. You cannot underestimate the stress you might feel, especially as you will be living this 24/7. There is a real danger of trying to take on the world all by yourself. There can also be an impulse to isolate yourself socially while you focus on the task of getting your life back on track, but know it is far healthier to speak out. The issues to consider here are:

- **Life Continues:** Life does not stop because you don't currently have a job. People, partners, and friends will continue as normal. Work is after all just one compartment of our total lives, albeit a very important one.
- **Support:** The strength and support your loved ones will provide you are of real comfort, not to mention the ideas and inputs they can provide to any approaches or presentations you may use as part of approaching a job application.
- **Personal Narratives:** The stories we tell ourselves can shape the realities of our life and circumstances. Be mindful to keep positive and focus forward to change your current reality.

Practical Steps and A Plan of Attack

Consider your value proposition, what you seek in a role, and how you'll effectively promote yourself and to whom. Segment your network in terms of immediate opportunity, introductions to decision-makers, and longer-term activities. Coffee and cocktails are going to be your battleground here. Always ensure you are being a good servant to your network at all times, because the more you give, the more support and help you will receive when you need it most.

Review Your Career Journey

If you are starting from scratch, it's essential to update your CV or LinkedIn profile. If you're out of practice with interviews and self-promotion, now is the time to focus on this. Getting comfortable discussing your skills, motivations, goals, approach, accomplishments, and what makes you stand out is crucial. You need to have your perspectives and responses well-rehearsed and ready to go.

We will build on this section later in the book and particularly with exercises to assist you to identify and build your brand, approaches, and philosophies in Chapter 15: Optimizing Your Personal Brand. For now, you need to ask yourself a series of questions and have prepared answers for them. This is key to crafting the compelling stories that will make the strongest case for why you are the right hire. More on this topic is within Chapter 11: Dust Off Your Best Stories and Your CV for Best Impact. Begin to consider and map out the following:

- What has been your career journey so far?
- What skills and experience do you have?
- What is your WHY? What motivates and drives you?
- What are your career goals? Where are you now and where would you like to be in 3 to 5 years' time?
- What are your approaches and philosophies toward your role or function?
- What do you care about passionately, what are you best at, and what got you into your current industry?
  - By chance or design? if chance, did you learn to love it and why?
- What have you learned that you would pass onto others?
- What do you dislike?
- What have you accomplished (business growth, delivered efficiencies, sales, learning, audience development, mentoring, etc?)
- Address your LinkedIn profile, review/update/change/highlight your achievements.
- Think about why you left positions.
- What is the state of the job market?

- Where will you source jobs?
  - Network (personal and professional).
  - Companies you know personally.
    - Review how you are connected to these.
  - Recruiters, who?
  - Jobs boards and social networks.
- What is your minimum expected salary and benefits package?
  - Work out your ranges for searches and interviews, you have to be ready and comfortable to speak about money.
- Practice speaking about your roles and experience.
- Consider what stories will back up your applications.
  - Hone and practice these. Make sure they are reflected in summary within your CV, LinkedIn, and other outreaches.

Other Considerations

Do not forget to address the fact that you will have more time on your hands and how best to use this. Consider your mental health and relationships as well as your monetary position.

- Address your monetary position:
  - How long can you budget for?
  - What costs can you cut?
- What will be your daily routine?
  - Where will you work?
  - When will you work on applications?
- What will you focus on in the downtime?
  - Learning, exercise, hobbies, family and friends.
- Consider your network:
  - Develop a personal brand on social media.
- Resilience:
  - Consider how you will handle rejection.
  - Adapt your mindset and prepare for what can be a lonely battle to get recognized.

- Support:
  - Speak to family.
  - Are there friends or colleagues who could support you in finding opportunities?

Thinking about the questions and points above is all about preparation for action. There is admittedly a lot here. The fact is, for many of us, our circumstances may not be ideal when confronting this situation, and work is a massive part of our lives which can affect us in all aspects of our lived experience. Taking a holistic view is to ready yourself and to ensure you are in peak condition to accomplish what you need to. This is a moment, perhaps an extended one, but temporary. You will create the opportunities, and you will bring into your life the people and conversations that will help you to get to where you need and deserve to be. Armed with answers to these points you will already be on course to making the most of a targeted approach to your job hunt. An additional benefit is that you will have affected a mindset focused on selling yourself, (yes that term again!) in the best possible light. You will have also begun the preparation for face-to-face interviews by considering some of your motivations, strengths, and approaches. Remember, be strong and be positive. This circumstance is not you, and it won't define you.

Letting Go Lightly

It can be hard to move on if you have your mind fixed on a company or a role. However, only one person can get any job and as unpalatable as it may be to consider, it may not be you, despite all the effort and passion you have directed toward the cause.

Of course, you must prosecute every opportunity with every fiber and element of your focus, but, should you not get the desired outcome, you must be able to both learn from the experience and ultimately let it go, for it was not meant to be, and you still must find what it is you are looking for someplace else. Become the master of your uncertainty to refocus your fears and your energy to fight the long campaign.

Building Resilience

Fear is highly connected to our brain function, which signals danger to the rest of our body initiating the fight, flight, or hide modality. The danger is that our capacity to think is literally shut down and that we can spiral into non-action and even depressed states. Within any campaign, you will have to manage your resources, which includes managing yourself. Be prepared to be resilient and work at ways to maintain a positive goal-focused mindset. Do not let your fear limit either your vision or the opportunities that you might otherwise have created for yourself.

Having a clear objective and set goals aligned to a program of activity, both for work and physical fitness, will help keep your spirits up and mind occupied. There will always be darker days and uncertainty, but the more you are focused on bringing into your life the people, goals, and circumstances that you desire, the more that you will be able to manage the times when you are feeling less confident. Staying resilient through difficult times and focused on a goal requires a combination of mental, emotional, and practical strategies. Perseverance is crucial for maintaining consistent effort and motivation over time, even when progress seems slow or obstacles arise.

Takeaways

- *If made redundant, do acknowledge that this could be one of the hardest experiences of your life, depending on your circumstances.*
- *Plan and prepare in a holistic way with the goal of being ready for interview.*
- *Strike quickly within your network to try and quickly find possibilities.*
- *Frame your current situation positively. Create your future outcomes and bring into your life the people and circumstances that you need to be successful.*

CHAPTER 6

LinkedIn and Building a Powerful Presence

Chapter Summary

- Your LinkedIn profile is your online CV. From your profile picture to your content, ensure that it is portraying you as you wish to be seen.
- Understand how your LinkedIn presence is used by recruiters. Leverage key words for screening visibility and position these well.
- Your entire digital footprint could also be considered to be your extended résumé.

LinkedIn has become such an important factor in the world of talent, recruitment, and job hunting that we need to spend some time to focus on it, and what it means to us from a candidate perspective. By better understanding this platform, you can hope to get the most out of it and to use it for your advantage in the job market. This chapter will cover profile hygiene and basics. Once you have an optimized LinkedIn profile, we will look at how to use your LinkedIn effectively as part of your networking strategy. Let's start with the LinkedIn basics and why it's such an important tool for your professional life.

Key Steps to Optimizing Your Profile

Optimizing your LinkedIn profile can significantly enhance your visibility and attractiveness to potential employers and professional connections. I will use my LinkedIn profile to help illustrate elements, not because it is perfect, but because it will hopefully serve to illustrate the points I am making. No doubt there are areas whereby I can improve. Indeed, even in writing this, I am conscious that it might be a good time for a review, and this is also the point I would like to impress upon you. Make sure that your profile does correctly and accurately reflect your current and future vision of yourself. Your development and growth will never be static, so ensure that your profile does not reflect the past and that you keep updating your skills and experiences accordingly. To begin with, ensure that you are using good imagery:

- **Professional Profile Photo**: Use a high-quality, professional head, or body shot. Do not use a photo from a night out with someone's cut off arm in the photo. It is not a good look. Cartoon or avatar images can also work, particularly in some industries. Also consider that profiles with photos receive far more engagement than those without.

- **Background Image**: Make sure you utilize this space and put something important to you there. If you are a public speaker, you on stage would be a great idea, otherwise you can use imagery that demonstrates your focus, industry, or your company. As you can see, I have been drawing attention to my first book, *The Cultural Sales Leader*, but in the future I may want to change this depending on my focuses.

- **Compelling Headline**: The next key area to work on is your headline. Maximize the headline as it should be more than just your current job title. Highlight your expertise, skills, and what makes you unique. This is a critical element, as it is one of the first things people see. This is where recruiter and sourcing centers will be noticing used keywords. You may well be the "VP for Business Development," but if that is all you have, you will miss recruiters searching for more specific terms such as "Fintech," "Payments," and skills such as "Management" and so on. Be concise, be exact. Do not waste space, and make it truly reflect you and where your career journey is headed. (Figure 6.0)

You can see from my profile that I currently have a leg in two worlds. My intention here is to draw attention to my books and thought leadership, however, I am also actively known in the payments world as a commercial leader. When it comes to leadership, I have some specific ideas and focuses, and I want to highlight that I am a "people-first leader," hence, "servant leadership" is important to me when building winning cultures. Please give this section some careful thought and think about ways to concisely tell your story.

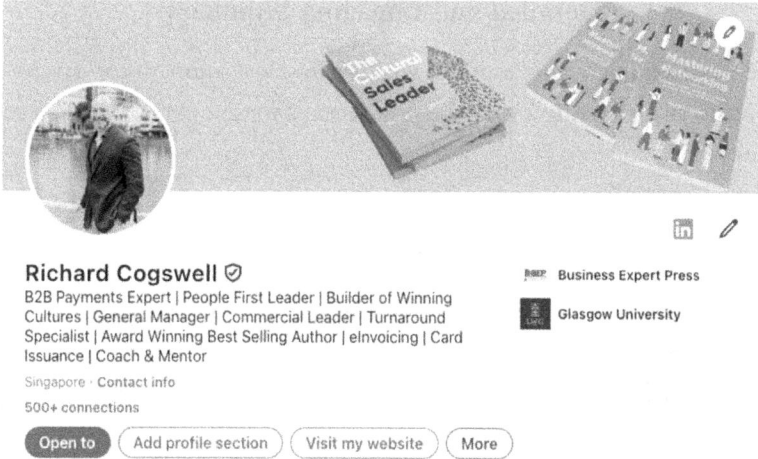

Figure 6.0 LinkedIn profile example

Custom URL: As with any social media, make sure you personalize your LinkedIn profile URL to make it more memorable and professional. For example, mine is https://www.linkedin.com/in/richardcogswell/. *If you are reading this, let's connect! Let me know what you think about the book!*

Next Steps

Congratulations! We are already making great strides along the way to creating your outstanding LinkedIn profile which will attract more interest and opportunities. Now we get into the details of your résumé, your current and past positions, achievements, skills, endorsements, and learnings.

It is at this point that LinkedIn starts to resemble the traditional CV. Remember, this is your publicly available calling card. The world will come and find you, so make sure it serves you well. Profiles with limited information will be passed over by recruiters and sourcing centers. Do not simply list companies and schools, instead, expand on your experiences, as you would on your CV. Embrace fact-based self-promotion and share your accomplishments aligned to the value you offer, showing your potential to contribute.

Detailed and Engaging Summary

Write a summary that captures your professional journey, key achievements, and what drives you. Use first-person narrative to make it personal and engaging.

Headline Optimization

Your headline is one of the most visible parts of your profile and crucial for keyword optimization. Include job titles, industry-specific terms, and key skills. For example:

- **Before**: "Project Manager at XYZ Corp"
- **After**: "Project Manager | PMP Certified | Agile & Scrum Expert | IT Project Leadership"

About Section

Here you can draft a compelling summary about yourself and your career. This can be in the form of a narrative that highlights your experience and skills. Make sure to include both specific and broad terms:

- **Example**: "*As a seasoned **Project Manager** with over 10 years in the **IT industry**, I led **Agile** and **Scrum** teams to deliver successful **software development projects**. My expertise includes **stakeholder management**, **budgeting**, and **team leadership**.*"

Activity Section

This section publicly details your last posts, comments, videos, images, and articles. This should become a section you focus on when networking.

Experience Section

Flesh out this next section to cover your working achievements to date in your career.

- **Showcase Experience and Achievements**: List current and past positions with details of your roles, responsibilities, and achievements. Quantify your successes with metrics to provide concrete evidence of your impact. Detail your roles with action-oriented language and include keywords related to your skills and achievements. Use bullet points for clarity. Be snappy to accommodate quick profile scanning.
  - **Examples**:
    - *Managed end-to-end **project lifecycle** for multiple **IT projects**, ensuring delivery on time and within budget.*
    - *Utilized **agile methodologies** to improve team efficiency and project outcomes.*

Projects and Skills

Add relevant skills to your profile and seek endorsements from colleagues and clients. This enhances your credibility and highlights your expertise. Endorsements are effectively recommendations or references you can call on when new employers are doing their due diligence on you. Include relevant certifications and educational qualifications, using the full names and acronyms.

- **Examples**:
  - PMP (Project Management Professional).
  - Certified Scrum Master (CSM).
  - Bachelor's Degree in Computer Science.
  - Agile Methodologies.
  - Risk Management.
  - Stakeholder Management.
  - IT Project Leadership.

Recommendations

Request recommendations from former bosses, colleagues, managers, or clients. It really does add credibility. Make sure you continue to ask for these as you progress on your journey. Recommendations that mention key skills can also boost your profile's visibility.

- ○ **Example:**
  - ▪ *"John's expertise in **agile project management** and his ability to lead **cross-functional teams** were instrumental in our project's success."*

Interests and Group Memberships

Join LinkedIn groups related to your industry and areas of expertise. Include any volunteer work or interests that highlight your personality and values, as this can make your profile more relatable and well-rounded.

- ○ **Example:**
  - ▪ Groups: "Project Management Institute," "Agile and Lean Software Development."

By implementing the strategies above, you can create a compelling LinkedIn profile showcasing your professional brand to attract opportunities through better recruiter search optimization.

Keywords Optimization

Refining your profile with key search words involves strategically placing relevant terms that recruiters commonly use in their "Boolean searches."

Boolean Sourcing and Why You Need to Know About It

The days of a recruiter working alone with their network to find talent for open positions are long over. Now many recruitment companies are working with what is known as "sourcing centers," teams of people using advanced search techniques to gather a "talent pool," or long list of potential candidates, who they then approach to screen for requisite skills and availability for a role.

A Boolean search allows users to combine keywords into search strings as a method to refine and improve results by using logical operators such as AND, OR, NOT, to produce more relevant and targeted results. You must know this so that you might maximize to the best extent possible your LinkedIn profile to ensure that you are spotted for the attributes that are important to you and your professional journey.

The primary Boolean operators include the following:

1. **AND**: Narrows the search by combining terms. All terms must be present in the results.
2. **OR**: Broadens the search to include results that contain any of the terms.
3. **NOT**: Excludes terms from the search, filtering out unwanted results.
4. **" " (Quotation Marks)**: Searches for an exact phrase.
5. **( ) (Parentheses)**: Groups terms or operators to structure complex queries.

Talent sourcers use Boolean search strings to refine their search queries within LinkedIn to find profiles that match specific criteria, such as job title, skills, location, industry, and experience levels. They can then use filters to narrow down search results and focus on candidates who meet their requirements. For example, a sourcer seeking junior-level software engineers, might use the following:

"(software engineer OR developer_ AND (Java OR Python) NOT (senior OR manager)"

Such techniques are particularly effective if there are specific skills required, such as high demand, or specialized skills, particularly when there is the requirement for hiring at scale. Recruitment Process Outsourcing (RPO), or Managed Service Provider (MSP), programs are examples.

They are also used for smaller-scale specialized recruitment fronted by an individual recruiter or headhunter.

RPO Programs

An RPO is a large-scale permanent recruitment program, managed for a hiring company by an outsourced recruitment agency. In other words, with this program, a company outsources all its full-time, permanent hiring process. In this instance, a hiring company likely has a larger volume of full-time or permanent hires to make on either a periodic or full-time basis. Here, the outsourced recruitment partner will assume all or part of the company's recruitment functions. In this respect, the RPO provider acts as an extension of the company Human Resources (HR) or Talent Acquisition (TA) teams, managing all aspects of the recruitment process on their behalf. These programs are highly sought after by the global recruitment firms.

MSP Programs

An MSP is a freelancer or "contingent" workforce solution. Hiring for temporary or contract workers can be scaled per market or for project-based requirements. Construction is a great example of an industry, which utilizes MSP heavily.

Roles Most Suited to MSP and RPO

Certain roles are particularly well-suited due to their high demand or specialized skills. Some examples could be:

- **Technology and IT Roles:** Software engineers, data scientists, UX/UI designers, and cybersecurity specialists are frequently sourced by recruitment sourcing centers.
- **Sales and Business Development Roles:** Entry to midlevel sales, business development and account management roles, typically in industries such as software-as-a-service (SaaS) and other technology or professional services sectors.

- **Engineering or Manufacturing Roles:** Mechanical engineers, electrical engineers, project management professionals, and manufacturing technicians for a whole host of industries, such as engineering, infrastructure projects, automotive, aerospace, and consumer goods.
- **Healthcare and Life Science:** Nurses, physicians, pharmacists, and biomedical researchers are often targeted by recruitment sourcing centers, particularly for healthcare organizations and pharmaceutical companies.
- **Finance and Accountancy Roles:** Recruitment sourcing centers may focus on candidates with expertise in such areas such as financial analysis, auditing, tax accounting, and corporate finance.
- **Customer Success and Support Roles:** Recruitment sourcing centers may target these professionals for roles such as customer success managers, technical support specialists, and customer service representatives or call center personnel.

Using Keywords Effectively

Some considerations to think about:

- **Research Keywords**: Use LinkedIn job postings and job descriptions to identify commonly used keywords.
- **Consistency**: Ensure that the keywords you choose are consistently used throughout your profile.

Here are some examples of LinkedIn keywords to use (this is by no means an exhaustive list), also ensure that you use and promote skills, including soft skills, within your keywords, depending on your industry or role:

- **For Marketing Professionals:**
  - Digital Marketing.
  - SEO Specialist.
  - Content Strategy.
  - Social Media Marketing.

- ○ Brand Management.
- ○ PPC Advertising.
- ○ Email Marketing.
- ○ Marketing Analytics.
- ○ Growth Marketing.
- **For IT/Tech Professionals:**
  - ○ Software Engineer.
  - ○ Full-Stack Developer.
  - ○ Cloud Computing.
  - ○ Cybersecurity.
  - ○ Data Science.
  - ○ Machine Learning.
  - ○ DevOps.
  - ○ Python/Java/C++ Developer.
  - ○ Artificial Intelligence (AI).
  - ○ Blockchain.
- **For Sales Professionals:**
  - ○ Business Development.
  - ○ Sales Enablement.
  - ○ Account Management.
  - ○ B2B Sales.
  - ○ CRM Systems (Salesforce, HubSpot).
  - ○ Lead Generation.
  - ○ Sales Strategy.
- **For Project Managers:**
  - ○ Project Management.
  - ○ Agile Methodology.
  - ○ Scrum Master.
  - ○ PMP Certification.
  - ○ Risk Management.
  - ○ Stakeholder Management.
  - ○ Process Improvement.
  - ○ Resource Allocation.
  - ○ Cross-functional Leadership.
  - ○ Change Management.

- **For Human Resources (HR) Professionals:**
  - Talent Acquisition.
  - Employee Engagement.
  - HR Strategy.
  - Recruitment.
  - Performance Management.
  - Training and Development.
  - Diversity and Inclusion.
  - Compensation and Benefits.
  - HR Analytics.
  - Organizational Development.

Engagement on LinkedIn

Well done! You have your basic LinkedIn profile in operation. Now you need to start to get the platform to work for you. This means establishing yourself as an engaging voice on meaningful topics. Post and share content related to your field using relevant hashtags to increase your visibility and reinforce your expertise in those areas.

By sharing insights, achievements, or industry trends, you position yourself as a thought leader while fostering engagement with peers, clients, and recruiters. Focus on content that provides value, such as actionable tips, lessons from experience, or commentary on current events in your field. Post while at events or tradeshows to draw connections and potential customers to you. Use authentic storytelling to connect emotionally and display your expertise. The outcomes can include heightened visibility, stronger professional relationships, and opportunities like career advancements, collaborations, or leads for business growth. LinkedIn's algorithm favors active profiles, increasing the chances of your posts being seen by a broader audience. Remember to use hashtags and also to tag others where relevant (Figure 6.1).

The image below shows you the analytics page on your LinkedIn profile and is a handy place to keep on top of your posting activities and the results you are getting. It's also a section you should research when preparing for meeting others.

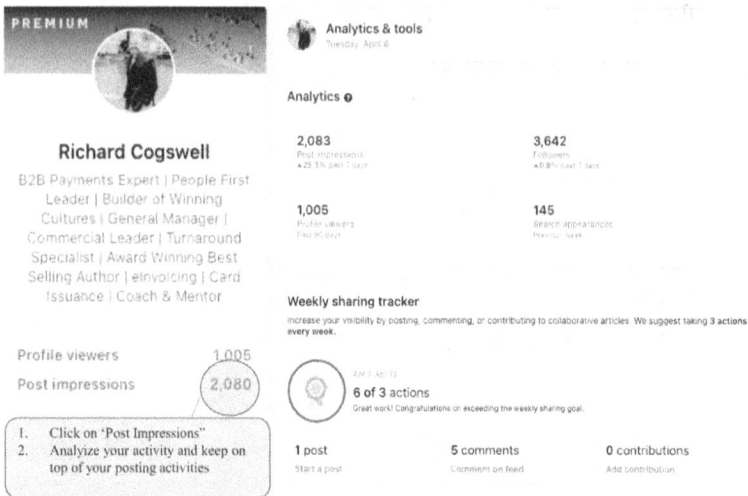

Figure 6.1 LinkedIn engagement analytics example

Components of Your Digital Footprint

I read a post recently on LinkedIn that suggested that the CV is dead and that your professional résumé is now your entire digital footprint. That got me thinking.

Your digital footprint is significant. When researching a prospect, I recommend taking a broad approach to uncover insights that can help you make connections and steer interview conversations to your advantage. Keep in mind what works for you also works for those hiring you. Publicly available information is exactly that, so be mindful of what you share. It is important to separate your public and private profiles. Here is an overview of what this includes and the potential risks of not keeping your social and professional profiles distinct:

- **Professional Profiles**:
    - ○ **LinkedIn:** Your profile is the central pillar of your professional digital footprint, so make sure that you spend time on getting it right and that you update it often so that it most accurately reflects today's version of you.
    - ○ **Online Portfolios**: Personal or business websites or platforms where you display your work, or interests, such as GitHub for

developers, Behance or Fiverr for designers, or personal port-
folio sites.
- ○ **Professional Associations**: Memberships and contributions to
professional organizations, which may have online directories
or profiles.
- **Social Media Profiles**:
  - ○ **Facebook, Instagram, Twitter (X)**: Personal social media
profiles where you share updates, opinions, projects, side gigs,
photos, and interact with friends and family. Consider running
both public and private versions of these.
  - ○ **YouTube, TikTok**: Platforms where you may share video content that reflects your personal interests or hobbies, perhaps
even business interests.
- **Publications and Media Appearances**:
  - ○ **Articles, Blogs, or Whitepapers**: Written work or thought
leadership pieces you have published.
  - ○ **Interviews or Podcasts**: Appearances that showcase your
expertise, opinions, or personal insights.

Implications of Not Segregating Social and Professional Profiles

Mixing personal and professional content online can lead to several issues, including privacy concerns and reputation management challenges.
Exposing personal information or views unaligned with your professional
image can unintentionally affect how you are perceived. Without clear
boundaries, your online presence may become inconsistent, making it
harder to establish a strong, cohesive professional brand. Personal posts
or comments could be viewed as unprofessional, especially when placed
alongside career achievements, potentially damaging your credibility and
job prospects. Additionally, having a mixed audience can create networking challenges, as professional contacts may be uncomfortable with personal content, while friends and family might not appreciate professional
updates. Employers often search online during candidate screenings, and
unprofessional content found on personal profiles could negatively influence their perception of you, regardless of your work qualifications.

Keeping personal and professional content separate is essential to managing your privacy, reputation, and job search success.

Best Practices

Consider then the following as best practices for your overall online image.

- **Separate Accounts**: Maintain separate profiles for personal and professional use. Ensure that your LinkedIn and professional profiles focus solely on your career and achievements.
- **Privacy Settings**: Use privacy settings to control who can see your personal social media posts and manage visibility according to your comfort level.
- **Consistent Branding**: Ensure that your professional profiles are consistently branded and reflect your skills and experiences accurately.
- **Regular Reviews**: Periodically review your digital footprint to ensure that all content aligns with your current professional and personal goals.

By properly managing and segregating your digital footprint, you can enhance your professional image while maintaining your privacy and personal interests.

Takeaways

- *Build your LinkedIn professional profile to optimally reflect your experience and skills.*
- *Understand keyword search optimization and ensure that your profile is showing correct and consistent terminology.*
- *Think about an engagement strategy for building and interacting with your network.*
- *Be mindful of your overall digital footprint and ensure it reflects the impression you want to convey.*
- *Ensure you review and update your profile regularly.*

CHAPTER 7

Degrees of Connectivity, How to Network Effectively, and Being a Good Servant to Your Network

---

Chapter Summary

- Your professional network is your greatest asset in both your job search and career.
- Think of your network as a sustaining entity, one that you need to build, nurture, and serve as much as take learnings and opportunity from.
- "Dig the well before you thirst."

Degrees of Connectivity

We bring into our lives the people and circumstances that we dwell upon.

Attributed to Ralph Waldo Emerson,
American essayist, lecturer, and poet

Like it or not, we are all connected, even more so than in the past, especially with the advent of the internet and social media. We have many opportunities to develop and build our networks by extending our reach to other industry professionals.

- **In Person:** Good old-fashioned face-to-face interactions rule. Any tradeshow, conference, or social event you go to is potentially a networking opportunity.

- **Digital:** Digital networking platforms have transformed the way professionals find one another, access content, connect and interact. They have facilitated conversations on a scale, scope, and speed that were unimaginable in the past. This global reach facilitates broader networking opportunities and collaboration across geographical boundaries, compared to the more localized networking of the past.
- **Specialized Communities:** Tailored to specific industries, disciplines, interests, or career goals, providing valuable opportunities for networking, knowledge sharing, and support among professionals with shared interests.
- **Pre-Meeting Research:** Meeting someone for work or socially? Check out their LinkedIn profile as part of your preparation for the meeting. This not only allows for better conversations but also offers an opportunity to connect in the professional space.

You may not realize it now, but your next job opportunity, your next raise, your next promotion and advancement in your industry, they're already there, waiting for you to come find them.

Still, despite the ease, networking can seem daunting for many. Fears of rejection or assumptions about lack of expertise or having nothing compelling to offer, can be at the crux of this, but it can also be due to social anxiety, perceived inauthenticity, time and effort investment, negative past associations, or concern about networking etiquette.

The truth of the matter, according to the "six degrees of separation" theory, is that any two people in the world are connected by, on average, six acquaintances. If you look at this in the context of networking for career advancement, this means that individuals are typically only a few connections away from someone who could potentially influence their career for the better. Therefore, by any measurement, your network is an incredible asset to leverage through targeted efforts. Those who do can increase their chances of connecting with influential people to produce potentially life-changing meetings that open the door to new career opportunities.

The Benefits of Networking

I have gained value from my extended network on several occasions, including the following:

- Helping in hiring decisions.
- Deciding on career moves and job offers.
- Finding talent.
- Helping to learn or upskill in a particular area.
- Giving back by helping to introduce others to critical contacts for many of the same reasons.

Growth and participation in your network is not just about your current goals in securing new opportunity. It is much more than that. Look beyond the present and build your voice on topics that matter to you. Consider how you can actively contribute to serving your network, boosting both your career growth and visibility through:

- **Access to Opportunities:** Networking provides access to a wider range of job opportunities, including as we have discussed, those not advertised, granting access to the "connected job market."
- **Insider Information:** It's about differentiation and using all the tools you can bring to bear. The game is not rigged, but you need to maximize your chances. Through networking you can gain privileged insights into industry trends, specific job roles and opportunities, company cultures, hiring manager focuses, leadership styles, current challenges at the hiring company, and so much more! It's a total waste not to reach out to people who can help you differentiate in a hiring process!
- **Personal Recommendations:** Building relationships through networking increases the likelihood of receiving a personal recommendation or referral to a role or hiring manager, which can significantly increase the likelihood of you (a) getting to interview and (b) getting the job.
- **Skills Enhancement:** Learn from other's experiences and post your own to connect, exchange knowledge, and gain valuable

advice and mentorship. The more you give, the more you will get in terms of enhancing skills and expertise.

- **Increased Visibility:** Actively posting and participating in networking events, industry conferences, and gatherings can raise your visibility within your professional community, making you more recognizable to potential employers and future collaborators.

- **Career Support and Guidance:** Providing opportunities for receiving support, guidance, and feedback from peers and recognized industry professionals, helping you to navigate career challenges and make better strategic and career decisions.

Overcoming Networking Fears

For many of us, there is a real hurdle to overcome when considering a room full of potential connections. Some are wired to be more naturally gregarious than others, and much of this comes down to social anxieties that can be heightened in a work or professional context. The good news is that it is possible to learn how to overcome these barriers, and much of it is about being authentically you. At the end of the day, human connection is key. Networking and social interaction is also like a muscle. The more you exercise and develop it, the easier it becomes, and it genuinely becomes FUN. I am a salesperson, but you might be surprised to learn how many of us either identify, or used to identify as introvert. Often, the very best salespeople are in fact those that might admit to a weakness on the social side of things.

Social awkwardness can be a significant barrier to effective networking, especially for introverts who may feel overwhelmed by the prospect of large gatherings or initiating conversations with strangers. However, introverts can overcome these fears and become exceptional social connectors by embracing their natural strengths, such as active listening, empathy, and authenticity.

Instead of trying to mimic extroverted behaviors, introverts can focus on building meaningful one-on-one connections where they can engage deeply and genuinely. By being authentic and human in their interactions, introverts can forge strong relationships based on trust and mutual respect. Thoughtful questioning and active listening can leave a lasting impression on others. Over time, these more intimate, authentic interactions can help introverts grow into confident, powerful networkers who create meaningful and lasting connections.

Networking can be perceived as daunting for several reasons:

- **Fear of Rejection:** A common reason is the fear of rejection or the concern that you might be imposing on the other person. This can also stem from feelings of inadequacy or thinking someone is "out of your league", too knowledgeable or senior to approach.
- **Social Anxiety:** For some people, social interactions, especially with strangers or in a professional setting, can trigger feelings of anxiety or discomfort. The pressure to make a good impression and engage in meaningful conversation can be overwhelming.
- **Lacking Confidence or Imposter Syndrome:** Confidence plays a significant role in networking success. Individuals who have limiting beliefs about their abilities, or those who feel insure about their professional value, may struggle to initiate conversation or be able to promote themselves effectively.
- **Social Uncertainty:** Perceived unwritten rules or etiquette can be intimidating, not knowing how, and indeed, when to approach others, what to say, or how to follow up can create avoidance and reluctance to engage at all in networking activities.
- **Perceived Inauthenticity:** Some may think networking is somehow insincere or about personal gain rather than genuine connection. First connect, and second, look for opportunity. Learn how to be curious and interested in the moment. Being authentic is about being yourself, don't overcomplicate it. Learn how to focus your interest and questions on the other person and wait to be invited to speak about yourself. Remember to follow up afterwards to continue the dialogue.
- **Time and Effort:** Networking takes time, effort, and persistence. You must make yourself available for opportunities. Building up and maintaining any relationship takes sincere effort. This may feel daunting if your schedule is already busy, or if you have many

competing priorities. If this is the case, focus on the outcomes you wish to create and prioritize accordingly. Set and follow realistic goals.

- **Negative Experiences:** Every now and then you might come across someone rude or dismissive, but it is exceedingly rare. Part of this is also learning how not to outstay your welcome. Do not let any bad experiences affect your enthusiasm for putting yourself out there to broaden your connectiveness within your professional life. Always review and assess what went well and where you can improve.

To address all these concerns, you must reframe your mindset. Honestly, the greatest confidence you can build is through experience. Practice and celebrate the little wins. Each successful engagement or meaningful conversation should help you realize there's nothing to fear. If you are still struggling, then seek support and guidance from mentors, or from those who seem to do the work well. Do not be afraid, for example, to ask an expert networker just how they do what they do and ask for tips or suggestions. Always focus on building genuine, mutually beneficial relationships, rather than viewing your networking and, by extension, your network as a transactional activity or resource. Insincerity or leading with demands will quickly lose you connection.

Overcoming Fear of Rejection or Imposter Syndrome

Overcoming fear of rejection and social anxiety in a professional or networking environment requires a combination of mindset shifts, practical strategies, and gradual exposure to social situations. Here are some steps to help manage and reduce these fears:

- **Reframe Rejection:** Rejection is a natural part of life, especially in networking (this is part of taking a more sales-minded approach to your job hunting. Rejection is a common feature of sales, and you simply have to get used to it. Instead of seeing it as a personal failure, view it as feedback, or simply part of the process. Not every connection will work out, and that's okay.

- **Focus on Value**: Build confidence by focusing on your skills, experiences, and what you can offer to others. When you recognize your value, social situations become less about impressing others and more about mutual exchange.
- **Accept Imperfection**: You do not need to be perfect. You simply need to be authentic. Social and professional interactions don't require flawless communication. Authenticity and a willingness to engage are far more valuable than perfection.
- **Gradual Exposure**: Begin with smaller, low-stakes social interactions to build confidence, such as one-on-one meetings, and gradually work your way up to larger events. Try non-pressured lunch dates with colleagues you do not know so well, for example.
- **Prepare Ahead**: For networking or professional situations, prepare a few conversation starters, questions, or topics related to the event or industry. Having these in mind can reduce anxiety and help you feel more in control.
- **Use Active Listening**: Shift the focus from yourself to the other person by asking questions and listening attentively. This not only takes the pressure off, but also makes the other person feel valued, fostering a more comfortable interaction.
- **Use the Environment for Openers**: If an event has speakers, you can make call back to a point of interest or a raised topic. Even asking simple questions about the environment such as, "*Who is that?*" "*What is that?*" and "*What did you think of?*" can open remarkable conversations. Avoid tired approaches such as, "*Where are you from?*" "*Where do you work?*" and "*What do you do?*" Challenge yourself to ask such questions only once you have already learned something about the individual you are speaking to.

Challenge Negative Thoughts

- **Negative Thought Patterns**: Anxiety often arises from negative self-talk, such as assuming people will judge you, or that you will say the wrong thing. Challenge these thoughts by reminding yourself that most people are more focused on themselves than on criticizing others. Maybe even make a feature of this!

"I'm so bad at these events!" could be a natural and honest opening that could bring the other person's experiences and feelings
into play. Imagine if the person said, *"Ha-ha me too, I used to be
dreadful at these events and never knew what to say,"* now you have
the perfect opportunity to ask how they adapted and what they
have learned to be great techniques over time. Suddenly, you are
having a very human conversation.

- **Visualize Success**: Instead of focusing on what could go wrong,
  visualize positive interactions and successful networking experiences. This can help create a more optimistic and relaxed mindset
  going into the event.

- **Keep It Human**: I cannot tell you how many times I have
  got into incredible conversations with folks only to learn later
  who they were and what they did. Let me tell you, had I asked,
  "What do you do?" up front, I may not have done so well. When
  you find out that someone is a CEO of a huge multinational,
  the chances are you might clam up, or try too hard to make the
  conversation professional, with the chances of coming across as
  dry and boring. Treat people as people first. We are all, at the end
  of the day, social animals. An entertaining conversation around
  topics or concepts or side issues such as the city you are in, what
  you are eating, what their motivations for being at the event are,
  what they have learned, and so on, will engage someone and help
  them connect to you far more readily than the usual discussion
  about what they do for a living.

- **Groups versus Individuals**: It can be intimidating to break into
  a group at an event, so speak to individuals in your lunch queue
  or at coffee breaks by joining those standing alone.

Be Kind to Yourself

Understand that overcoming social anxiety is a journey. Celebrate your
progress, no matter how small, and be gentle with yourself when things
don't go as expected. Incorporate relaxation techniques, such as deep
breathing or mindfulness, to help manage anxiety before and during
social interactions. By taking small, manageable steps, embracing your

authentic self, and keeping it human, you can easily become more comfortable and confident in professional networking environments.

Figure 7.1 Networking is not so hard

Build Network Before You Need It

Dig the well before you thirst.

Attributed to Chinese Philosopher Confucius

As with anything, define your starting point and then build your strategies from there. To find out your current following, check the current number of connections you have on LinkedIn. Scroll to your LinkedIn analytics, click "post impressions," and find the "audience" tab. Here you will find out how many "followers" you have. LinkedIn no longer makes a distinction between connections and followers in terms of the size of your network. Another thing you can do is check your "Social Selling Index" (SSI), this is a score that LinkedIn will generate based upon four critical activities:

1. Establishing a Professional Brand.
2. Finding the Right People.
3. Engaging with Updates.
4. Building Relationships.

A Google search on "find my SSI score on LinkedIn," will bring you to a page on Sales Navigator to find out your score. All of the above represents your complete professional network in digital terms, today. You can follow this up on other social media, such as Instagram and others should you wish to, but let's focus for the purposes of this book on the professional side of things. It is never too late to start building your network. Start with colleagues, past and present, customers, leaders, recruiters, friends, and others who you already know. Pay attention to the "My Network" tab on your LinkedIn for further suggestions of who you might add to your audience and network.

Of course, it is better to have made a start and to be focusing on further growth. In today's professional landscape, the power and potential of a network is more significant than ever before. Networking enables individuals to connect directly with decision-makers, bypassing gatekeepers and creating relationships that lead to job referrals, partnerships, mentorships, and collaborations. In many cases, opportunities arise not from what you know but from who knows what you know. A well-connected network can amplify your visibility and credibility in your industry.

You Already Have a Network

The best starting point is to identify your readymade network and to then find who can help you today on your candidacy journey. Consider this as actively using your network to gain valuable insights and support, enhancing your overall effectiveness and success. Having people you can bounce ideas off for feedback on your journey is vital, and this is all the more powerful if your network is diverse.

When networking, do not be afraid to ask for time with anyone, no matter how senior, but do be clear on why you are asking and what you hope to gain from the meeting. When reaching out to somebody for the first time, be compelling in your outreach and state your goals clearly. If they match those of the person you are approaching, then so much the better. Coffee, lunch, or cocktails are all learning environments where you can gather inputs or perspectives on an issue or challenge. One introduction can lead to another and so on, until you find yourself discussing potential roles.

Curating a winning outreach is all about research, helping you to pen a mutually compelling approach. Beyond the usual LinkedIn and social searches, think in terms of searching for any articles or posts that you can use to build the connection and mutual interest quickly.

Your Existing Network

- **Executive Sponsors:** Leverage your existing and past reporting lines by connecting with the leaders you have worked with, expanding your network through second and third degree connections. Additionally, build relationships with senior leaders, both within and outside your organization to extend your reach, gain support, and gather insights for the conversations you want to initiate.
  - Just unpacking a challenge or an issue with someone experienced, interested, and not directly in your day-to-day reporting line can be a helpful way of identifying useful next steps and actions to help resolve or progress your cause. In this interaction, asking more broad questions about the person's experience in handling a situation would be more advisable than going into heavy detail.
- **Friends in Commerce and Industry:** Ensure you are keeping across macro factors that might be affecting your industry and the wider opportunities presented. Maintaining connections with friends in business is valuable for potential collaboration, knowledge exchange, opportunities, and the cultivation of a supportive professional network that can contribute to mutual growth and success. Bear in mind the power of internal referrals to hiring processes.
- **Experts:** Cultivate a learning mindset. Seeking market, product, or customer base experts provides the opportunity to learn and improve about how you talk about propositions, products, and services.
- **Professional Coaches and Mentors:** A mentor is someone you form an informal relationship with, either within or outside your

current organization, to guide career development. A coach, on the other hand, can be an informal or professional paid relationship that helps you refine your approach to work and enhance your skills.

- ○ Be bold and use these contacts not only for introductions but also for ideas and feedback on your proposed outreach, whether that be to potential hiring managers or to recruiters. Having an impartial set of eyes on your content can be a powerful thing. Also, and if you are not so confident with self-promotion, use these sounding boards to make sure that you are elevating your value and that you are not falling into common errors such as being overly wordy or aggressive in your outreach.

- **Your External Network, Customers, and Partners:** These are people who you have worked with and who know you and can be great supporters.
- **The HR Community:** Consider targeted connectivity to HR at the firms you are most interested in joining. Through these connections, you will also find your way into the searches of other connected HR professionals, recruiters, and headhunters.

Networking into a Role

When you find you are closing in on a contact who could be important to a career conversation or when you are about to meet someone in interview, use your network to find out more about them and the company or job on offer. Never be afraid to ask for time with someone, no matter how senior, but do be clear on why you are asking, and what you hope to gain from the meeting. When reaching out to somebody for the first time, be compelling in your outreach and state your goals clearly. In this respect, it always pays to be super concise. Consider that the person on the other side is busy and will likely only see your message when on the move. If you imagine them between meetings, this should help you to craft something clear, to the point, and with an ask. For example, *"Hi [contact's name], I hope this message finds you well. I know you through our mutual connection [colleague's name]. I would value the time to discuss [topic and reasons]; would you be free for a coffee at [location and time] next week?"*

Set your goals. For example, you might manage to get an audience for half-an-hour with someone connected. That's not a great deal of time, especially if one of you is late. Also bear in mind there will be small talk *"How do you know so and so?"* and so on. You might also be queuing for coffee, for example, with broad conversation about how long you have been living someplace or how long you have been in the industry or working at a company. Once you do sit down, your 30 minutes is maybe 20. So, what's your goal? I, for example, would have a simple objective, just get to the next conversation with the next influencer in the hiring chain.

How to Connect with People Through Your Network

When networking to secure a meeting, a more thoughtful approach is essential. You can either reach out directly or use an intermediary, but one tool stands out for this purpose, email. Email is the most effective communication method, offering a direct, professional way to connect and is more likely to yield a response than other tools. While LinkedIn's InMail feature can be useful, many users don't actively check or respond to messages there. Over time, you'll also notice that some LinkedIn profiles aren't as engaged, so while InMail can still be a part of your strategy, focusing on direct email will typically deliver better results. How to find email addresses is covered in Chapter 8.

We are all connected through only a few degrees of separation. On LinkedIn, you will see whether a prospect is a first, second, or third degree connection. Connections are organized by degrees representing the levels of familiarity and distance between users in the network. A first-degree connection is someone you are directly connected to because you have accepted their invitation, or they have accepted yours. A second-degree connection is someone connected to one of your first-degree connections. You can connect with them by sending an invitation, and LinkedIn will show you their profiles to encourage networking through mutual contacts. A third-degree connection is one step further, someone connected to your second-degree connections, making them more distant. This structure helps users leverage mutual connections to expand their reach. No one is beyond the reach of your network. Let's look at the process to connect with someone, and let's assume that this prospect is a senior business leader who you wish to approach to discuss potential opportunities. We will use the connectiveness method to leverage your existing network to gradually reach the desired contact.

The "Prospect"

Clearly define who it is you want to connect with and search for them, then review their profile. Pay special attention to how many mutual connections you might already have in common, this can be a great opener if you are going direct. If not mutually connected, look to potential second and third-level connections through whom an introduction could be made.

Prospect Research

Gather as much background as you can on their professional journey and their interests. I know some of you may feel ill at ease regarding this topic, but think of it as the politest thing you can do. Think of how you would feel if a stranger reached out to you without any awareness of you, your work, or your interests, and they then asked for some of your precious time to pick your brains over coffee. Not the most enticing approach. Do not think of people in an impersonal manner. Do not consider them to be targets, or stepping stones. Always think in terms of how you would like to be treated. Look to highlighting their work, a mutual connection, or an alignment to a topic of interest. If you emphasize this in your approach, you are more likely to think of creative ways to connect with them on a human level.

What I'm not suggesting here is anything intrusive or overly aggressive in your networking efforts. Instead, to capture someone's attention and secure their time, you need to either offer value or tap into a shared passion or interest. That's the goal. Through the steps outlined below, we will focus on identifying those common threads, ideally passions, that can spark meaningful dialogue. After all, wouldn't you prefer to work with people who align with your values, behaviors, passions, and philosophies?

The obvious place to start researching is LinkedIn and their profile, which will tell you about their schooling, professional journey to date, networks, career interests, and what content they have posted or shown interest in. Extend this search to the web and research whether your prospect has published any articles or posts elsewhere. Perhaps, there are interviews or other mentions of their professional journey out there:

Person'sName + Article + Blog + Interview + Post + Corporate/CompanyName

Make sure that you check out Twitter (X), Facebook, or personal blogs/websites. Searching beyond LinkedIn can not only provide unique insights into how to engage based on shared content, but can also offer a deeper understanding of who they are as individuals. For example, discovering which football team they support. Sports, hobbies, and passions often act as great levelers, breaking down professional barriers and creating opportunities for more authentic interactions. I would draw the line when it comes to restaurants, bars, or travel you might have in common at this early stage, as this may seem a little too intrusive, unless their pastimes are a significant part of their online persona, of course. If clues are limited, if their online footprint light on detail, then never fear. Just be professional and courteous in your outreach and impress on them your desire to learn from them over a quick coffee or drink.

Securing an Introduction

Start with those people closest to you and your intended prospect. Explain your goal and ask if they could help to connect you. Be clear about what you would want from the introduction. For example:

Hi [contact's name],
I hope this message finds you well. I'm reaching out because I'm interested in speaking with [business leader's name], for a quick coffee to discuss [topic or industry]. I would be keen to discuss:
  - *Topic one*
  - *Topic two*
  - *Topic three*

Given your connection to [business leader's name], I wonder if you might be able to help facilitate an introduction? Thank you so much and let me buy you lunch sometime this week to thank you.
Best [your name].

Make sure to highlight any mutual interests or goals that could make the introduction more appealing. Sometimes, it helps the intermediary if you suggest some wording they can use, for example:

Hi [intermediary name],
Thank you for helping with the introduction to [business leader's name]. Here's a brief message you can use if it helps: "Hi [business leader's name], I hope you are well. I wanted to introduce you to [your name], who is [brief description about you]. They are interested in [specific topic, or discussion points]. They have some great ideas and insights on [relevant topic], and I thought it might be valuable for both of you to connect over a beer or a coffee [as appropriate]. I believe a conversation would be mutually beneficial, best [intermediary name]."

In this way, you are being grateful, courteous, and you are also potentially saving them some time, while also reminding them to make the connection for you. When you do see the email or note passed, then be sure to respond, making sure of course to thank your connection for their support.

Follow the Chain of Introduction

Politely follow through on each lead. Always honor the fact that your network is being generous by expressing gratitude for any assistance you may receive. Never chase folks. This is a huge turnoff. Also do not send messages that allow for no action, or that can be easily ignored. This is a fine line to trace sometimes, but a good rule of thumb is to always be conscious of how you would feel in the interactions you put out there. Try to pay forward or assist in return, if asked.

Going Direct

If contacting a prospect directly, craft a concise and compelling message to request a meeting:

Dear [prospect's name],

I hope this email finds you well. My name is [your name], and I've been following your work, particularly your insights on [specific topic], which I found truly inspiring. Your recent thoughts on [specific post/article], really resonated with me, as I've encountered similar experiences with [brief mention of outcomes].

We also share mutual connections, including [individual's name], who shares our passion for [topic/industry]. I'd greatly value the opportunity to meet for a coffee to discuss a few specific topics, including [list briefly], or your thoughts on [topics].

I look forward to meeting you.

Best regards [your name].

Adapting Your Goal

The goal in any outreach to a dream company, hiring manager, or role is always to get the job. Acknowledge, though, that while this is the ultimate destination, the first outreach is step one of many steps along what could be an exceptionally long journey. First off, you will need to get into the vision of the potential hiring manager. Then you will need to navigate HR, the interview process itself, and any tests and stages specific to the role or position you are applying for.

You are therefore not fighting one fight here. You are fighting a campaign, and campaigns can take time and can have setbacks, delays, and other frustrations. Adapt your mentality and goal setting accordingly, so that you do not lose energy or become frustrated along the way. Think incrementally about how you will set yourself up for success, and you will protect your mental health and energy in the process. Incremental gains as an idea refers to the process of making gradual and continuous improvements, so, instead of fixating on the result, change your perspectives:

- What is the goal of this email?
  a. *To get to the next conversation.*
- What is the goal of this meeting?
  a. *To get to meet the next person in the process.*
- What does success look like for me after this conversation?
  a. *To better understand the hiring landscape, to know more about the challenges faced by the company, to test my assumptions, and to get to a point where I can summarize my application, strengths, skills, and focuses to provide real value in role.*

Also think about what is in it for the intermediary. Yes, you want the job, perhaps desperately, but limiting the aperture of focus on your ambition can result in you achieving more, long term. By doing the above, you are getting very specific to the moment, and you will always be maximizing your research and preparedness for each step of the way. You will also turn up to each moment more focused, energized, and optimized to perform. Let's say you have secured half-an-hour with someone senior at a company, this is a golden moment and you do not want to simply go in and wing it. Make sure you do your research and prepare some topics. Also rehearse your lines. Remember, there will be moments where you must think on your feet and respond in the moment. Role-playing your side of the conversation will allow you to handle these freestyle moments with greater ease and grace when they come.

Information is power when making career decisions, allowing you to both qualify yourself in or out of opportunities. You have always the power to say no, or that in hindsight this is not for you. Qualifying yourself out of an opportunity allows you to refocus toward where you want to be. If you ever find yourself in this moment, get it out there clearly, thank the other person for their time and inputs, and do not fear it. The other person will also appreciate your candor and potentially may even be able to help steer you in the right direction.

Remember that you cannot possibly know everything about a company and its culture, priorities, and challenges from the outside looking in. It is okay to be wrong. If you can substantiate or test assumptions by reaching out to connections on LinkedIn, then so much the better, but 100 percent accuracy is not the aim here. What I can tell you is that having made this effort, it is more probable that the interviewer will help to coach you, allowing you to hone both your understanding and your proposed actions and focus areas, thereby strengthening your case for hire even further. Just remember to be humble when expressing opinions or ideas on where you could help the organization with the maximum impact.

> *It is okay to be wrong on your assumptions about a company or role. Be confident in the fact that you cannot know all things at this stage looking from the outside in. This is about testing your assumptions and substantiating them in conversation. Coming prepared with insights or questions highly increases your chances to be coached for the role you are applying for.*

Once you have researched the company and prepared for the person you are meeting, practice your elevator pitch about yourself and your professional journey. You do not want to be under pressure when delivering these. Identify the skills, approaches, and outcomes you want to emphasize, in the context of working with or for the person you are meeting. With all this practiced, you will be more prepared, less nervous, and more able to concentrate on the dynamic factors of any conversation, the body language, the prompts, spontaneous topics and subjects that may come up.

Express Gratitude

After the interview, send thank you notes to the person you met and to anyone in your network who helped facilitate the connection. Give progress updates as well as you proceed. People have invested in your journey after all. This not only shows appreciation, but will also serve to strengthen your professional relationships for the future. Nothing is better than professional or life relationships where the both of you are pulling for one another and enjoy seeing each other win. Below is a sample thank you note you could consider adopting:

Hi [business leader's name], thank you so much for taking the time to speak with me today. I truly appreciate your insights on [specific topics discussed]. Your advice will be incredibly valuable when I meet [next contact's name], and as I take the next steps we agreed upon [detail or information of how you plan to use the information]. Best Regards [your name].

Here is a sample update note for the introducing intermediary you could consider using:

Hi [intermediary's name], thank you once again for introducing me to [business leader's name]. Our conversation was incredibly insightful, and we have agreed the following [detail next steps or individuals you are set to meet]. I'm so grateful for your support and could not have done this without you. I'll keep you posted as things develop. Let me know if I can help you in anyway, now or in the future. Best [your name].

By following these steps, you can strategically navigate the connected job market and build relationships with key individuals, paving the way for informal conversations that could eventually lead to formal job opportunities.

Common Mistakes

I am sure we can think of overtures made by others who want something from us more than they want to make a genuine connection. Our inboxes are full of approaches demonstrating no research or sensibility of whether we have any interest in what is being offered. Messages can be overly broad and reflect a lack of thoughtfulness or effort on the sender's behalf, such as "*Please help me find a job at your company.*" Others might be overly "salesy" or aggressive, demonstrating a lack of EQ. Additionally, overly verbose messages often fail to capture attention and can come across as careless or inconsiderate of the recipient's time. We, too, would prefer to avoid receiving this type of outreach. Repeatedly attempting to grab attention is not an effective strategy for building meaningful connections.

You may well be passionate, and you may well desire to see yourself at a company. None of that inherently grants you any right to a conversation. People are busy, and the timing and circumstances related to hiring may not be in place, hence, your outreach might be seen but not necessarily acknowledged. If you do get a reply thanking you for the submission but stating that the timing is not right, be thankful, and make a point that you will follow up within a suitable timeline. Companies do not move as quickly as you might assume or want. Getting attention is one thing, but be cautious of being cheesy, smarmy, or overly familiar, err instead on the side of being passionate and compelling. Keep it short and elevate the impact and points you are making so that someone busy can absorb, summarize, and take on your message. That's all you are looking for at this stage. The ultimate goal is the job. The incremental step is the next conversation.

Remember, a network is not something you should simply lean upon, it is something you must also serve. Being a good servant to your network will ensure that you will in turn receive support when you need it.

Practical Tips When Networking

The best advice I can give you is to always be prepared within a networking environment.

- Have your stories well-versed in terms of introduction, focuses, and what you hope to learn or gain from the event you are at.
- Connect as people first, businesspeople second.
- Do not be afraid to connect. Be prepared to initiate and swap LinkedIn details (Figure 7.2) and always follow up.

Ensure you set all this up before entering a networking situation, and, at the appropriate moment pull out your phone and ask, "*Shall we connect?*" This is so much better than a card, as you are guaranteed a live connection. The other person will likely read your summary (which is why it needs to be compelling and to the point) and then you will find yourself already in easy conversation. Make sure you follow up after connecting with a thank-you note or a message to continue the conversation.

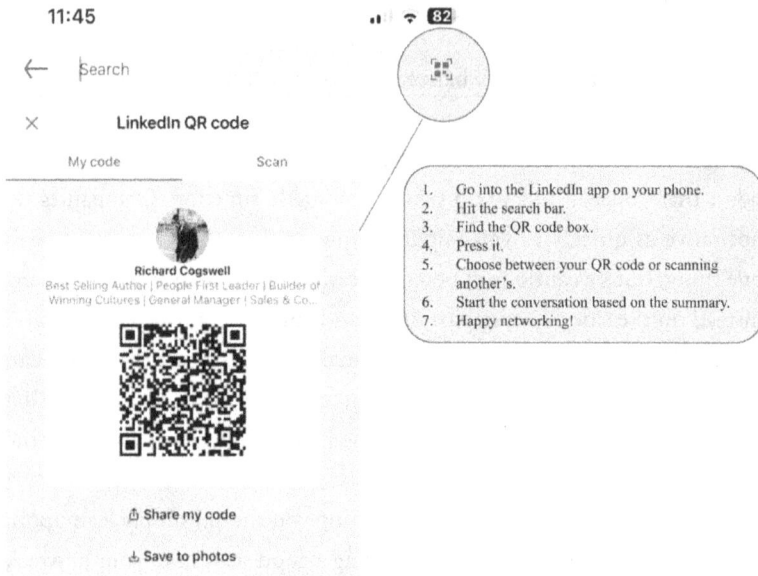

Figure 7.2 Where to access your LinkedIn connection QR code

Networking Etiquette

Just as you would want a friendship to be based on mutual trust, respect, and generosity, so should you think and act that way toward your network. Trust and perception are the cornerstones of meaningful relationships. When your actions consistently reflect care and consideration for others, without ulterior motives, trust naturally grows, deepening mutual respect.

However, relationships become fragile when generosity is only extended when convenient, or when you approach others only in times of need. Constantly asking for things without giving back erodes the authenticity of the connection, making your intentions seem self-serving.

The best way to think about your network, therefore, is as a living, dynamic ecosystem that thrives on mutual support, collaboration, and shared value. Rather than viewing your network solely as a resource for personal gain, think of it as a collection of relationships built on trust and reciprocity. By contributing to others' growth and success, you strengthen foundations. Your network can open doors for you when you nurture it by investing in people, giving before receiving, and fostering two-way value exchange.

Ultimately, a well-maintained network can be one of the most valuable assets for a professional, acting as a bridge to both immediate and long-term success.

Being a good servant to your network means consistently offering value, support, and genuine engagement, without expecting anything in return. It involves taking the time to listen, understanding the needs of others, and offering help where you can, whether by sharing relevant resources, providing thoughtful advice, or connecting people to new opportunities. A servant mentality requires a mindset of generosity, where you actively look for ways to uplift others and contribute to their success. It's about building trust and cultivating meaningful relationships through authenticity and selflessness, recognizing that by helping others, you create a thriving, mutually beneficial network built on reciprocity and goodwill.

Your network is not just about posting your work updates, promotions, and activities. These are important of course, as they serve to give an insight into your professional progress as well as help shine a spotlight on your expertise. Beyond this, think of what you would most want in a coaching or mentoring relationship and try and bring that mindset to posts. This could involve sparking discussions around experiences or sharing advice by telling stories and lessons in an engaging manner. The best and easiest way you can do this is through joining the conversations on authored posts. You will see plenty daily on your LinkedIn feed. Do not be concerned by the stature or title of the post's author, believe me, they want engagement, and they want to spark dialogue and debate.

Pick a thread close to your heart and rather than just "liking," or praising, add a point of view. Remember, the key to this is to always be compelling and to add an opinion, or experience. Compose something, reread it, hone it if needed, and do not hesitate over the post button, send it! Reply to likes and responses by deepening the dialogue. Once you have done this several times and built confidence, think about a topic or topics you might post about yourself.

In many cases, opportunities arise not from what you know but from who knows what you know.

If you follow this simple progression, something interesting is going to start happening. Your network will begin to grow, not just in size but also in quality. People are naturally drawn to those who are supportive, authentic, and reliable. Word spreads about individuals who provide value without strings attached, and you'll often find that new connections come to you through interaction with your posts.

Servanthood has the capacity to create a ripple effect. When you help one person succeed, they are more likely to introduce you to others who can benefit from your expertise, creating a cycle of mutual benefit. While you should never give with the expectation of receiving, your contributions to others will often come back to you in unexpected and meaningful ways. This is because people want to support those who have supported them. When you consistently offer your help, others will look for ways to return the favor, whether by sharing opportunities, providing referrals, or helping when you need it most. People are more likely to go out of their way to help you when they've seen you do the same for others. This mutual exchange creates a vibrant, engaged community of professionals who are invested in each other's success. Over time, the depth of these relationships leads to sustained career growth, access to new opportunities, and a broader range of resources and knowledge.

Practical Ways to Serve Your Network

Below are some practical examples to consider:

- **Posting:** Contribute to posts and create your own posts. Do not copy, but do think about your topic, who your audience is, or even what you are in opposition to, as a way to kick off your contributions.

- **Offering Support:** Proactively seek opportunities to assist others in your network. This could involve providing advice, making introductions, sharing resources, or suggesting pathways to those seeking them, aligned to their goals and needs.
  - When I first turned to authoring books, I was very green and inexperienced. In truth, I went about my first book in entirely the wrong way! One of the elements you must cover off is asking for permissions to quote other authors or works. I reached out to the publishing company for one of my quotations and received nothing. As we were getting close to publication, I wrote directly to the author herself, a multi-*New York Times* bestseller. Not only did she reply personally, graciously providing permission, but she embarked on a correspondence that was filled with encouraging insights that have helped my journey enormously. You'll be surprised how many will help, if you present your request in a compelling way!
- **Be a Connector:** One of the most valuable things you can do for others is to connect them with people who can help them grow or achieve their goals. Whether it's introducing two colleagues who might collaborate well, or connecting a mentee with a mentor, you become an invaluable resource by helping others form meaningful connections where people could benefit from knowing each other.
- **Expertise and Advice:** If someone in your network is facing a challenge or needs advice in your area of expertise, offer to help without expecting anything in return. Sharing your knowledge builds your credibility and strengthens your relationships.
- **Provide Resources:** If you come across an article, podcast, book, or tool that could be helpful to someone in your network, share it with them. This shows you are thinking about their needs while staying engaged with their professional development.
- **Celebrate Successes:** Acknowledging the achievements of others in your network is a powerful way to show support. Whether congratulating someone on a new job, or a promotion, taking the time to celebrate their success fosters a sense of camaraderie and mutual respect.

- **Be a Mentor**: Offering mentorship to those who are earlier in their career is a fantastic way to serve your network. By sharing your experiences and providing guidance, you not only help others grow but also reinforce your own expertise while expanding your influence within your industry.
- **Check In**: Maintaining relationships requires ongoing effort. Reach out to your network periodically, even if you don't have a specific reason. Simple check-ins can keep connections fresh and show that you care about the relationship beyond transactional needs. Do not be that person who is only checking in when they need to.
- **Support When It Is Least Expected**: Offer help even when it's not asked for. If someone in your network is going through a tough time or seems overwhelmed, extend an offer to help or to provide encouragement. This kind of support demonstrates empathy and creates bonds that last far beyond professional interactions.
- **Follow Through:** Honor your commitments and follow up on promises made to your contacts. Whether it is providing contacts, assistance, making personal introductions, or offering support, reliability and accountability are essential for building trust and credibility.
- **Express Gratitude:** Show appreciation for support and guidance when received. Acknowledge the contributions of others and express your gratitude often.
- **Be Genuine and Authentic:** There is no trick to this. Just be your true self.

Finding Your Tribe

Networking does not mean connecting to *everybody*. It is not simply a numbers game. The most successful networking is intentional and authentic. It requires a genuine interest in others, a willingness to help, and a long-term mindset. You should bring an attitude of service to your network. It is not simply a resource to take from. Building strong relationships over time leads to trust and reciprocity, creating a dynamic where opportunities flow naturally.

The long-term benefits of servant leadership within your network are profound. As you continue to serve others selflessly, you create a network of individuals who view you as a trusted, reliable, and generous partner. This trust will pay off in countless ways, people will refer business to you, offer you job opportunities, recommend you for promotions, and advocate for you when you are not in the room. Your reputation will spread, attracting even more opportunities and connections to your professional world. When you help others succeed, you naturally become a leader in your community, someone who others look up to and trust.

Takeaways

- *Do not be afraid to reach out to your network for introductions, information, or to test your assumptions and approaches to others, but do be sensitive to people's time and how much you are asking of them.*
- *Never be afraid to connect with and reach out to anyone. The more direct the better. Email is best, but do present a polished, compelling, and researched approach.*
- *Research and preparation are key, always.*

CHAPTER 8

The Advertised Route: Techniques to Enhance Success

Chapter Summary

- The focus of this book is on networking yourself into positions whereby you can create your own job opportunities. There, of course, remain the advertised roles. If you are going to apply to these, learn how to maximize your chances.
- Be conscious of where you are spending your time and what results you might get.
- Anecdotally, only about 20 percent of LinkedIn job adverts will be truly open processes.

The game is not rigged, but the odds do need to be tilted in your favor.

This book is about reducing reliance on traditional job boards and the standard application processes that typically accompany them. I was having lunch with a headhunter the other day who suggested that only about 20 percent of LinkedIn job adverts are truly open processes, meaning where there is not already an identified shortlisted candidate. It's hard to be exact about this number, but consider the number of posts on LinkedIn speaking of very few responses from hundreds of applications.

That said, you never know, right? This chapter will cover techniques you can consider when applying to a traditionally posted job advert. As we have covered, you are up against it when simply relying on this approach to the job market, so you still want to focus on differentiation, more so, because the recruiter will be receiving so many applications.

To get anywhere in the process, you need to ensure that you are showing up well and rising to the top of what is likely to be a large pile.

Clues in the Job Advert

You will soon find that there are two types of job advert. Those you can turn to your advantage and those you cannot. What do I mean when I say those that you can turn to your advantage? Those that supply clues that you can investigate and use to enhance your application, potentially to even break and turn the recruitment process to your advantage. What we are trying to do here is get to the hiring manager directly to ensure that they insist on your inclusion in the process, while making a differentiating impression compared to other applications by showing initiative and a tailored, researched approach to their role. If the role is truly open, you will have already stood out from the crowd. If it is not truly open, you will soon find this out. Overall, your chances of meeting the hiring manager are enhanced, allowing you the opportunity to gain feedback and introductions or ideas that will help you to get placed in due course.

I have followed these approaches myself, once to apply to a role at a large payments company. I bypassed the recruiter with a targeted one-pager of how I would bring my approach to role. The hiring manager reached out and we met. He told me that an internal candidate was already in mind but that my approach had intrigued him. Not only did I therefore not suffer the usual silence with no feedback, but I also forged a professional friendship that lasts to this day. As we have discussed, not every contact is going to bear fruit directly in terms of your being hired, but you will always be honing skills and developing your network. You can never underestimate how useful this is, or how it will help you long term in your career.

Types of Job Postings

The job adverts you will find will broadly fall into two categories:

1. **External Recruiter Job Postings.** Providing limited information.
2. **Direct Company Job Postings.** Providing nuggets of information that can be used to the candidate's advantage.

External Recruiter Job Postings

These are tricky, precisely as the recruiter wants to keep information tight to their chest. Remember that they are also competing with other recruiters, possibly with the hiring company itself. These corporates can be ambivalent to the external recruitment industry as the internet has, while not making the recruitment industry irrelevant, opened the path for candidates to find and apply for advertised roles directly, without the need for an intermediary. This, of course, saves the hiring company money.

Due to the openness of the internet and a competitive recruitment environment, recruitment companies no longer, or very rarely, have exclusive jobs to work on. Corporates, if opening jobs to the recruitment industry at all, will hedge their bets by working with several recruitment partners. This is also largely because these larger recruitment brands find it hard to differentiate among each other. All will claim similar capabilities. The individual recruiter has therefore got to be careful to protect the identity of the hiring company and the identity of the hiring manager. They will only bait the hook so much.

The point is that the recruiter needs to ensure that they have ownership of the candidate. If the candidate, for example, manages to register themselves directly with the hiring company, or with another recruiter, then the recruiter will lose their fee. I remember being fronted by three independent recruiters for a role, one who had contacted me and who I had declined 10 months prior to the role being reopened with a larger budget. When the role was reintroduced, several different recruiters contacted me, all as it turns out, for this same company and role. Each had been vague about the opportunity, so each time I was keen to explore. The issue was that I had submitted my CV via the original company, and now I found all fighting over my candidacy, when I advanced through the process. In some ways then, it is always a race for the ownership of the candidate. In these circumstances, the recruiter is suppressing information to protect their candidate flow to the hiring manager.

Here's an example job posting from a typical Global Recruitment company, (I have redacted some information but underlined the details that we can use to [a] identify the hiring company and [b] identify the hiring manager):

> About the company. *Our client is a <u>global leading MNC with a strong reputation within the Consumer Goods and Packaging indus-try</u>, servicing diverse industries including <u>F&B and the Chemicals industry</u>. Looking to drive their business forward within the region; they are looking for a <u>Regional Business Development Director APAC</u> to support growth for their <u>Plant Automation business</u> in the region. The successful candidate will be instrumental in expanding markets, developing business and sales strategies, and ensuring continued suc-cess within the region.*
>
>   About the job. *In this role, you will be collaborating closely with the <u>Global Lead,</u> to devise and implement sales strategies, directly leading to revenue growth for their <u>automation business in the APAC region</u>. The key markets covered will include the Food and Beverage and Chemicals industry. Some of the core duties of this crucial role include....* The advert goes on.

The advertised role above is a great looking Business Development role. We know this is going to be a heavily subscribed job. It's a senior position and a regional role with a global MNC, so we can assume it is a leading company. It also happens to have an attractively high budget in terms of package, (let's assume the advert went on to detail this). It's a peach.

However, the advert gives us little to go on. Underlined above are the key clues within this posting. If, as a candidate, you are interested in this role, you need to become the detective to follow down these clues to find out as much as you can to help your application stand out. However, the recruiter has done a great job of making this harder.

- The Company name is withheld.
- The Industry is obscured, sure, I can make a Google search us-ing MNCs in the automation business specializing in food and beverage, but I may not immediately pinpoint the company.

Sometimes you can get lucky, or perhaps I might produce several potential fits. Sometimes it's impossible. Cross-reference these company's careers pages to see if the role is there, which it may not be, especially if the role is new, or if there is still an incumbent in the position. The point here is you might have to simply apply blind.

- The hiring manager is not explicitly identified by title, you only stand a chance of finding this person if the company is identifiable to you.

The process here would be to make a broad Google search, such as:

MNC + Consumer & Packaging + Food and beverage + automation business + Leading Global Company

Let's say that your detective work does pay off and you have a target company now identified, now you must try and find the reporting line and the hiring manager. While the advert does not identify clearly who the role reports to, one can assume with an educated guess that a Global Sales Director or Head of Sales or Chief Revenue Officer could be potentials, and the only real clue you have here is that the role is a sales role and that you report and work closely with the "global lead."

All said though, good job recruiter! Not such a great advert for me the candidate. I'd say your chances of getting to the information you need is fifty-fifty at best. Many adverts give you even less information than this. In these instances, you can, of course, go ahead and respond to the recruiter and take your chances, but other than following up directly with the recruiter posting the job, (still recommended), there is not too much you can do if your Google searches come up blank on the company in question. You will be stuck in the CV pile, hoping you have sufficient experience on your résumé for the recruiter to shortlist you for a screening call. You may not even get a response. You will not know if the role is advanced in terms of valid applicants, and you probably cannot differentiate that much other than to ensure that your CV and your cover letter are as good as they can be.

Direct Company Job Postings

So, as discussed, these are the ones you want to try and get to more often. The reasons are simple:

1. The clues are easier to find and follow.
2. You can increase your chances of "breaking the recruitment cycle" to differentiate.
3. You can research more, and be better prepared for the coming interviews or meetings.

Direct Company Job Posting

Below is a small excerpt from a direct company job advertisement. Assume the hiring company is clearly identified, along with the requirements of the role, which is again for a Senior Business Development hire.

> …this position is based in [location] and reports to the Global VP of Business Development. The Vice President Sales & Business Development [location] is responsible for developing business in the local market and the general [region].

This advert is crying out for a differential approach. The critical elements are again underlined.

- Assume that we know the company and industry. You have the job title clearly mentioned. You know who this role reports to. You also know the region in scope. It is now easy to find this person and their direct email through a combination of searches. To do this, undertake a company search on LinkedIn within the country you are applying for, (alternatively, look for the HQ country. This example reports to a global role, and this person is likely based out of the corporate headquarters). Then click on people working at this company. Add a filter for the job title of the hiring manager. This may not be exactly as written in the job posting, so be prepared for that. The alternative is of course to Google search for the Global VP of Business Development at that company.

Read and reread the job advert carefully. Note the language used and also the key skills and competencies asked for. Pay attention to any cultural or personal traits the company is looking for. Companies often spell out something of the management or company culture within adverts, so look for these clues as well, you will usually find a company's values and mission statement on their website. For example, wording could indicate a startup environment with a fast-moving and rapidly changing culture. Here is your chance to highlight any startup or smaller company experience you may have. Companies calling for self-starters and those with an entrepreneurial mindset are usually pivoting with fluid goals and structure. The role is not likely to be intensively managed, so highlight your self-starter mentality and achievements within similar environments. To back this up, check resources such as Glassdoor.com, though be sensitive to the fact that disgruntled ex-employees might not be objective and may also be speaking about a past set of cultural circumstances that have since evolved.

Finding Email Addresses

Finding the Hiring Manager's email is a lot easier than you may think. Follow these steps:

- Use a LinkedIn Plugin. You will need to use the Google Chrome Browser for this. I personally use "Lusha" (https://www.lusha.co) though others exist, such as RocketReach. Some are free, offering a number of credits each month. Typically, you do not even have to expose the whole email as discovered by Lusha, (thus saving you search credits), as you are just looking to uncover the corporate part of the email address format. You can assume that the majority will be:
  - firstname.secondname@*corporateaddress.com,* with alternatives typically being *firstname@corporateaddress.com* or sometimes

more rarely *firstintial.secondname@corporateaddress.com*. If your email bounces, simply try one of the alternatives.

- If your plugin is drawing a blank and you are simply getting email rejections, enter a Google search as follows;
  Corporate Name + "Corporate Email Format"

  You will get a return from a site like http://www.email-format.com/ These sites will give you several suggestions ranking the most likely email format first.
- Still blocked? Cold-calling lives! With the described techniques, it's unlikely you will have to resort to this, unless you are in a country not well-served by these tools, such as Indonesia. In my experience, cold calling works well in such territories though, and you can usually get an email address with some persistence. Say you need to send an email, but you have the address incorrect, the person will usually then provide the details you need.

Having found your hiring manager's direct corporate email address, you must do some research to craft a compelling direct outreach for the role on offer.

Deepen Your Research

We have already covered some of what you can do to research a prospect and where you can find information in the previous chapter. Build now on all the information you have already collected through more company and role research. If they are a public company, discover how they have been performing by reading their shareholder reports and by seeing what the company executives are talking about in the press.

Seek out any social media blogs, articles, or posts that the hiring manager has engaged with (Figure 8.1) to get a sense of them, their philosophy, and what is important to them. To see what someone of interest has been passionate about, seek out the "posts" area of their LinkedIn profile to access a massive amount of information about their activities.

All activity

Posts   Comments   Images   Articles   Reactions

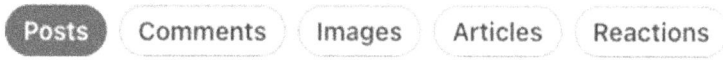

Figure 8.1 LinkedIn activity

All the tabs above will unlock potential talking points or areas for you to emphasize in your approach to this person. Pay special attention to the posts and comments sections as you can get an ear for their language and find real areas of similarity, focus, or interest. Understanding a hiring manager's philosophy is informative as you can get a sense of the culture you might be entering. You can also find people who have worked in your region and in similar or same roles and see if you can reach out to them to find out more about the environment, goals, and challenges, even information about the leadership style of the hiring manager as well.

Since all this is freely available, why would you not use information to be a better candidate, to be able to tee up better conversations and approaches? A personal bugbear of mine is how little research candidates do when going for interview, and there is no excuse for it. To not come prepared to take some control of the interview is the height of laziness and frankly shows that the candidate is not as committed as they could or should be.

An Arresting Outreach

Mention people you are both connected to, or people you know in the organization. If you have already spoken to them about the role, this is also worth mentioning. Highlight something about yourself that connects you to the Hiring Manager in some way. This could be an experience, a skill or a philosophy, which chimes with a challenge or topic you know this person is facing or interested in. Follow up with three to four carefully crafted bullet points that address a key element required of the role based on your reading of the job advert. These points should be short and punchy. Attach your CV and tell them you would love the opportunity to come and discuss the role with them. An example email might be:

Dear [hiring manager's name],

I hope this message finds you well. I recently came across your job advert on LinkedIn, [or mention discussions connected to the role] and was impressed by your leadership in driving [specific initiatives or outcomes the manager has led, based on your research, for example, "innovative customer engagement strategies" or "operational excellence at (company name)"]. It's clear that you are passionate about [specific value or goal, for example, "building a results-driven culture" or "fostering innovation"], I am inspired by the impact you're making in this space. As a [your role/profession, for example, "experienced sales leader" or "marketing strategist"], I have a track record of achieving:

- *[Specific, measurable outcomes, for example, "25% revenue growth through tailored client solutions" or "increased campaign ROI by 40% through data-driven approaches"].*

I believe that my expertise in [specific skills/areas, for example, "developing scalable strategies" or "cultivating high-performing teams"] aligns well with the objectives you are championing.

If you have time for a quick coffee next week, I would love the opportunity to discuss how I can support your vision and bring tangible value to your team, through:

- *[listed initiatives, approaches, philosophies, and outcomes].*

I'd be delighted to connect for a conversation at your convenience.

Best regards, [your full name]

Keep the message short and impactful in terms of the value, approaches, and outcomes you would drive, with some short examples. If you are then invited to email the HR, so much the better, as you can now cc the hiring manager and show connectiveness. If you get the coffee meeting, even better, you will have secured a vital moment to better solidify your understanding of the key elements and priorities. You will instantly be differentiating over the pack.

Takeaways

- *Go into advertised roles with your eyes open. Only a small percentage will be truly open. If you persist in going down the HR/Recruiter path, you will likely be disappointed.*
- *Study job adverts for clues that enable you to identify and then reach out directly to the hiring manager.*
- *Do your research and compile a strong outreach, your goal is to set a meeting or to be introduced to the HR through the hiring manager, thus establishing yourself in the process firmly.*

CHAPTER 9

Everyone Should Be a Salesperson. Find Your Sales Philosophy

Chapter Summary

- Be conscious of how much you might be holding yourself back and when you might be the obstacle to getting into hiring situations.
- Analyze and understand your relationship toward "sales" and "self-promotion." Become comfortable with the idea of proactively helping recruiters and hiring companies identify you as a talent they should be hiring.
- Be "hiring company first" in your thinking, preparation, and approach, not "candidate first."
- Do not be afraid of "stretch" roles. Use preparation and ROI approaches to counter fears.

Getting Comfortable with Sales

For a lot of people, "sales" can be a controversial term. The thought of "selling yourself" seems wrong, and people can have the connotation that it's boastful or overly "self-promoting." But essentially, the way I think about it, it's really about getting what you want, and what you deserve."

Richard Cogswell on The Career Changers Podcast
with Elisa Martinig, September 4, 2024

Are you one of those people for whom the very word "sales," or the idea that you might need to sell or self-promote yourself, creates sensations of anxiousness? Does the very term raise bad connotations, such as boastfulness or pushy behaviors? Do you recoil in horror and think about the common representation of sales and salespeople in the arts, in movies like, "Glengarry Glen Ross," or "Boiler Room," or do you think of the "Always Be Closing" pushy car or consumer electronics salesperson when the topic of sales comes up?

No one likes to be sold to in aggressive, opportunistic, and impersonal ways. It certainly does not help that this stereotype of the sleazy "car salesman" type is reinforced through our culture and in films and TV. What repels a lot of people is also the genuine fear of coming over as insincere or inauthentic. If any of that is true, then read on.

Everyone Should Be a Salesperson

This idea has been expressed by various business leaders, motivational speakers, and self-help authors. One notable advocate of this concept is Daniel Pink, a bestselling author known for his book, *To Sell Is Human: The Surprising Truth about Moving Others* (Riverhead Books, Copyright © 2012 by Daniel H. Pink).

Pink argues that in today's world, regardless of one's profession or role, everyone is engaged in some form of selling. Whether solving for client's needs or supporting an idea, or taking action, individuals are constantly influencing and convincing others in their personal and professional lives. The rationale behind this assertion is that effective persuasion and communication skills are invaluable assets in all aspects of life.

The ability to articulate your ideas well, present a compelling case for action, and build rapport with others can heavily enhance your success and impact. This is no truer than in the field of finding and securing career opportunities through your connected job market. Competition for hire is fierce, and attentions spans are short. The ability to "sell" oneself and one's ideas, therefore, is becoming increasingly vital for career advancement, business success, and personal fulfillment.

Adopting a salesperson's mindset, one that understands the needs and desires of others, enables you to communicate in a compelling and persuasive way. By fostering mutually beneficial relationships, you'll not only achieve your goals, but also make a lasting impact on your career path. This approach will set you apart, making companies more likely to hire you, regardless of the role or function.

Negative Perceptions of Sales

Still, negative feelings of sales abound. Many individuals view sales as somehow manipulative or pushy, associating it with sleazy tactics aimed at convincing someone to buy something they neither need nor want. Perhaps they have had bad experiences of cold calling or other forms of "hard selling," where it seems as if the entire exercise is simply to close a deal for the salesperson's benefit and not yours. Usually these approaches are cold, knowing nothing about your needs, desires, and values. Other reasons for negativity could be:

- **Fear of Rejection or Judgment:** Selling oneself requires that you put yourself in vulnerable positions with the potential for rejection or criticism. This fear could also stem from a lack of confidence in one's skills and experience. The truth is that it is very unlikely that you will face any form of criticism, especially if you have crafted a compelling and thoughtful outreach, however, our minds are adept at crafting visions of the worst of all possible outcomes, which leads us to procrastinate, or not take a step toward putting ourselves out there.

- **Modesty and Humility:** Some might be modest or humble by nature, but cultural norms and personal beliefs may also be at play. Even the way we are raised may discourage some from engaging in self-promotion. Some may feel uncomfortable or even guilty about drawing attention to themselves, or their accomplishments, preferring instead to downplay them. The danger is that these are not emphasized as positive proof points for hire. This can lead to non-proactive approaches with some preferring for others to come to them with opportunity. One cannot simply assume that others will note a person's impact, even should it appear obvious to the individual concerned. This retiring behavior also negatively impacts perceptions of leadership capability.

- **Imposter Syndrome:** A monster so many of us grapple with. People who suffer from this are usually more conscious about what they perceive they do not know, as opposed to focusing on what they do know. This can lead them to doubt their worthiness for roles and can manifest in the individual feeling or presenting as uncertain, without clear direction. It can also lead, in the worst of cases, to micromanagement or other more directorial styles of management. This lack of self-confidence can be a real blocker to either getting into hiring conversations or allowing people to effectively sell themselves in a recruitment process. If these individuals do not get advancement, this can appear to be a confirmation of their fears.

Self-Awareness and Small Improvements

If you are feeling any of these emotions or responses, I would take the time to note down what you are feeling and then try to diagnose why. The worst thing that you can do is to suppress or ignore the sensations. You can make substantial progress through a self-awareness exercise such as this. Rather than focus on seismic changes, focus on small changes to build confidence. Take the opportunity to practice in social environments, for example.

By focusing on the values and behaviors that drive your work, along with highlighting real, quantifiable outcomes, you'll be better equipped to respond confidently to questions like, *"What do you do?"* or *"How did you achieve this?"* This takes the conversation away from self and into a practical value-added conversation about technique, process, philosophy, and outcomes. Claims can be substantiated in fact and statistics. None of this is to brag, but it is to show competence and skills that apply to a desired role. Never assume that people will know in detail what you have contributed or brought to life in an organization, you must tell these stories. Practice alone or role-play, so that you develop your approach and stories before you try them out socially, this will also relieve a great deal of pressure.

The Definition of Help

Consider this definition from the *Collins English Dictionary*:

> *…to give or provide what is necessary to accomplish a task or satisfy a need; contribute strength or means to; render assistance to; cooperate effectively with; aid; assist."*
>
> Taken from the Collins Dictionary.com

Let that settle in for a moment. What is that a definition of? The above is a dictionary definition of the word "help." To be precise, the definition of "(help) transitive verb."

I am a lifelong salesperson, and this is the best description of sales I can think of. To me, selling is the art of identifying the customer's needs, ethically discerning whether a sale can be made at all, and learning how to relate to the customer, before presenting a solution in their language, matched to outcomes or returns on investment that resonate with their values and needs. If you can achieve this, then you will achieve positive outcomes for both parties. It is about being a trusted adviser. Is this not what successful candidates are also doing? To be a great salesperson, (or candidate), you need to differentiate. No one has clear and unobstructed access to markets or customers. Every market is crowded with competing solutions and companies. How you do what you do differentiates you, making customers more likely to buy from you. Differentiation is delivered through:

- **Expertise:** The best salespeople have a deep understanding of the space that they are working in and of the customers they are serving. This allows for the conversation to focus on learning the customer and then relating knowledge and solutions in a customer-centric fashion. Those salespeople who win most usually have done a better job of demonstrating that they have understood what the client is trying to achieve, so they might deliver the best ROI.
- **Approach:** People buy from people they trust and who are recognized for providing support, service, and value. If a

salesperson turns up underprepared, or speaks their language only (PowerPoint presenting, for example), or is pushy, rude, or overly salesy, then this is a turnoff. Those who turn up thoroughly prepared, who are expert in their topic or space, ask great open questions and actively listen, relay learnings back to the client in the client's language, and who present a solution to match the environmental needs they are addressing with clearly identified value-based outcomes will win.

○ **Trusted Relationships:** If the salesperson in question has delivered on the first two points and is responsive, knowledgeable, and fights for the customer, while demonstrating that their custom is valued, then already the beginnings of a long-term trusted relationship will be in place. If that person is pleasant to interact and spend time with, then the customer will have no issues turning to them as they need to. I know people, for example, who consistently buy their cars every few years from the very same salesperson for this very reason.

Reflect on the above and tell me, does that not sound a lot like what you are trying to achieve through interview? Imagine that you delivered all this before ever getting to the interview itself? That's what social selling is about. Let's break this down into how you could be adding significant value into the hiring process while simultaneously increasing your desirability as a fit for the hiring company. Consider the following actionable approaches to your candidacy:

• **Know Your Prospect:** Who is the hiring company? What do you know about them, their operating sectors and specific approaches to business? What are their cultural values and philosophies and how are they publicly manifested or spoken about? What is the role, its focus, the nature of the team, and how does it fit or interact with other parts of the business? What is the expected contribution and how is it managed? How do your approaches, philosophies, values, and behaviors impact and align with those of the business? What is the leadership style of your potential boss?

- ○ Candidates who are CV-led are less likely to be successful than those who will go in and have a conversation with the hiring company based upon research and the anecdotal insights they have brought from the market or similar companies, or situations they have worked within. Buyers' de-risk their purchases by buying from those that best understand them, and what they are trying to achieve professionally and personally.

- ○ **ROI**: Define the focuses and outcomes you will drive within 90 days, 6 months, or a year within role. Be clear on the measurements of success and how you convey those in the language of and for the understanding of the hiring company. Consider also, how do these results roll up to the overall outcomes and success of the business?

  - ▪ We sales folks like to call this the "opportunity cost" of not doing business. If there is a deal to be done, with a clear value proposition, then there is an opportunity cost to not proceeding. The same applies for your candidacy.

- **Authentic, Trusted Adviser**: What is the long-term relationship you hope to build with this company and why? Where do you see yourself in a year to 5 years' time? What will you have contributed and/or learned in this time?

  - ○ Remember, you are also interviewing the company in question, and you want to know where they will take you on your growth, learning and development journey.

For those of you uncomfortable with selling or self-promotion, and having absorbed the above, perhaps you can tell me what is either unsavory or challenging in the above descriptions and approaches. All you are doing is creating and delivering on a "customer mindset." Which is to say that instead of being "candidate first," you are approaching your hire from a "Hiring Company First" perspective. In summary, you want to be able to help the hiring manager to clearly and unequivocally see the value and benefit of your candidacy for the role on offer.

Confidence

Something I come across a lot is reticence to go for jobs that appear out of reach because of their title or seniority, or because there would be some form of learning needed to adapt and be successful in role.

The gender gap in applying for senior roles or positions that require a stretch beyond current experience is both perceived and real, for example. Studies show that women are less likely to apply for jobs unless they meet 100 percent of the qualifications, while men tend to apply when they meet only 60 percent*. This disparity stems from societal conditioning, where women are often more cautious about their qualifications due to concerns about perceived competence and imposter syndrome.

Unconscious bias in hiring and promotion practices can discourage women from going after senior roles. Despite efforts to address this gap, the challenge persists, with women often feeling they need to overprepare to be considered for the same opportunities as their male counterparts.

Source: "Why Women Don't Apply for Jobs Unless They're 100 percent Qualified" by Tara Sophia Mohr. Posted on the Harvard Business Review, August 25, 2014.

Confidence is the element I want to highlight. Confidence and taking a research-heavy, ethically high approach to stretch roles. Solid preparation, research and rehearsal can bring confidence for those struggling with self-promotion. You have nothing to lose in having a detailed conversation about where you are, where you want to be, and what that delta looks like. So many hiring managers I speak to (me included), are more interested in soft skills such as initiative, or a self-starting attitude than pure qualification for a role.

I recall one of the best hires I ever made in my career was for a technical customer-facing role where I knew I could not in any way help the candidate learn about the fundamentals of their role. I could assist on the client engagement piece, but what I needed was someone who would be able to source their own learning network, who could build and make the job their own, and who critically, could understand what was happening in a sales process and adapt their delivery to enhance a client's journey into our company's ecosystem. The ability to be curious and test and find solutions while building a supportive internal network was key to this individual's success.

A can-do attitude, initiative, passion, and a self-starting mentality can all out-trump experience if you need someone who can become and embody a role. These attributes can't be taught, and often, it's these foundational qualities that secure the job over someone with stronger qualifications on paper. So, never discount where you could be if you have an approach, a philosophy, values and behaviors that can get you ahead. You will always have experts in the business you are joining, and focusing on what you know is the key. You can find and learn from people who can give you the specifics over time.

> *If somebody offers you an amazing opportunity but you are not sure you can do it, say yes, then learn how to do it later.*
> Attributed to Sir Richard Branson, Entrepreneur
> and Founder of the Virgin Group

Embracing Uncomfortable Emotions

Growth often involves deliberate placing of oneself into uncomfortable situations. Think of the first time you spoke in a formal setting in front of peers or colleagues, for example. Stepping outside of your comfort zone is a powerful catalyst for growth and development, and it is essential if you are to become known for expertise in your space. Furthermore, it has the benefits of broadening your horizons, enhancing your skills, and building resilience. By gradually pushing your boundaries and embracing new experiences, you can unlock your full potential and achieve personal and professional growth.

This concept is rooted in the idea that stepping outside of one's comfort zone is fostering learning, resilience, and adaptability. Yes, investigating your emotions and fears might be uncomfortable, but consider them an opportunity to grow and enhance your candidacy appeal. When individuals purposefully expose themselves to challenges or unfamiliar territories, including internal reflection, they confront new perspectives, skills, and experiences that contribute to their overall development. The process of growing through discomfort is a deliberate and proactive approach to self-improvement. It's about recognizing that true growth often lies just beyond the boundaries of familiarity and complacency, encouraging individuals to embrace challenges as stepping stones toward becoming their best selves.

If you are using your job search for the purposes of advancement, you are likely embracing a growth mindset toward tackling challenges and obstacles through seeing them as opportunities for growth already. As popularized by psychologist Carol Dweck in her book "*Mindset: The New Psychology of Success*," a growth mindset is characterized as a belief that one's abilities and intelligence can be developed and improved through effort, learning, and perseverance.

Key to a growth mindset is the belief that abilities and skills are not fixed traits but can be developed and expanded over time. Failure and negative emotions are a part of the learning process. In contrast to a growth mindset, a fixed mindset is characterized by the belief that abilities and skills are fixed and that people cannot significantly change.

If you are struggling to fully embrace a growth mindset, a technique outlined in Chapter 10: Fear and Inertia, under the section "Negative Emotions," can help you to shift your predominant mindset and cultivate a more progressive approach. This is achieved through consciously addressing the emotions and feelings you are experiencing and interrogating them in a more positive way to identify solutions or actions. All it takes is conscious effort and practice, while finding the time to acknowledge and unpack each emotion.

A Sales Philosophy

The easiest way to get past any stigma in terms of sales or discomfort in the notion of "selling yourself" is to address and create your own philosophy of sales and selling. My philosophy of sales, for example, is entirely "people first." People have developed me in my journey, and, as a result, I aim as much as I can to help others on theirs, to the best of my ability. I see sales as being in the service of others and sales leadership being about helping others to be the best they can be in the attainment of their own professional and personal goals. Humility, a love of people, curiosity, ambition, laser focus, and a drive to learn, are all qualities I would describe as being components of the people-first leader.

If you do not have a guiding principle on what sales is to you, start by interrogating your personal values and build from there. Values are your core statements in terms of what is important to you and formulate a linkage between who you are as a person and how you show up to your profession. Refer to the exercise in Chapter 15: Optimizing Your Personal Brand.

Bringing It All Together

Hopefully, I have persuaded you to make the transition to be unapologetic in "selling." To practically apply a sales mentality to your job process, remember these basics:

- This is about knowing your customer (the hiring company).
- Knowing your product (you).
- Finding your passions (your drive to provide a winning solution. This is again, *you*, but more distinctly here, it is what *differentiates* you).
- Focusing on the ROI you represent to your function, to the business, via your approaches.

Your key mission is differentiation in a crowded market, so we must think in terms of value-selling. Always ask yourself, *"what value would I bring to the advertised role?"* and begin to work from there.

The Focus on Value

You bring unique experiences, values, approaches and thinking. How efficiently can you show these to a hiring manager? None of this is about bragging or self-promotion, this is all about **value**.

To show value, you need to know what the challenge is that you can solve for and then articulate why you are uniquely positioned to provide a fast ROI to the hiring company. As such, think of how to articulate your candidacy in terms of how you might solve problems, improve efficiencies, or contribute to the company's success through the context of your role. This approach involves in-depth research, personalized communication, and a consultative process. By demonstrating a clear alignment between your capabilities, experiences, and the company's goals, you will stand out, believe me, as you will build stronger conversations in interview, leading to stronger relationships, driving higher satisfaction and loyalty.

A non-threatening way to think about this and bring it to life is to identify your passions. These are the "whys" of you doing what you do. Most candidates think about or write about their roles and careers in the sense of "what" they do, which is literally a practical, dry description of role, function, and title. If you can shift to the why and then to the how of what you do as an emphasis, not only will you come across in a more compelling manner, but you will also begin to identify the value of what you bring.

Is Your CV Telling a Story, or Is It Merely a List?

Start with reading your CV, critically. Ask yourself, "does my CV currently read like a list, or can I see the achievements, the philosophy and the person?"

A list is factual, functional, and lifeless. A list is WHAT. If your CV reads like this now, it is an indication that you are also currently *thinking* in terms of WHAT you have done in the past. WHAT and HOW carry no emotion, no passion, and no sense of how you would be within a role.

Communicating in terms of WHY you are in a role or function indicates that you do more than just your job. For Hiring Managers, passion and initiative are like gold dust. They set you apart. Not only that, we all prefer to meet with interesting people, right? Look from the interviewer's perspective, someone who has articulated themselves from a WHY perspective should deliver a more enjoyable conversation. Sure, there are plenty who can do the job, but how many live it and will take the role forward with minimum management to the next level? Break your skills or previous job functions into their component parts and find what sparks of creativity you can and then begin to build on these.

This process will transform your performance at work as well. You should find it easier to speak about yourself and your experiences because emotional connectiveness drives dynamism born of excitement and animation. By injecting your thoughts on what a function is all about, how you would execute a role, or when you took something or someone to the next level, you are already beyond a formal job interview and now into a passionate conversation about something you believe in. Already you will have lifted yourself above the pack.

Making Your Passions Work for You

Get comfortable with thinking and talking about yourself in positive terms. If this is not within your nature, focus on the storytelling. Have an armory of stories you can use within your CV, cover letters, and interviews. Be authentic, be human, and be relevant to the type of role or function you are applying to. It's about showing something of what makes you tick and what motivates and excites you. It is also an insight into your execution of a role as well as to your other qualities as a person. Ask your friends or partner to help you hone and focus your initial thoughts if you become stuck or want to find better ways to express your points. You can role-play these in a safe environment that will make the entire process seem more natural.

Spend some time to write these thoughts down and to revise your CV with these principles in mind. Write down bullet points that pull out five or six statements that best describe you and your highest work or life achievements in the context of the roles you will be applying for. You will sharpen and change this over time and for each application, but get them down in a Word document you can access and use as the basis for your future applications. Not only will this save you time later, it will also give you a resource you can fine-tune and develop, which will allow these points to become even more powerful over time. Like a sauce, you will reduce the ingredients to amplify their impact and meaning. Maximize your language and use powerful assertive phrases. Think about the elevator scenario, whereby you meet someone and only have minutes to make an impression. Similarly, you must grab the interviewer's attention quickly.

Takeaways

- *Rethink your relationship toward selling and self-promotion.*
- *Differentiate: As a candidate for any role, you are competing within a very crowded talent marketplace of similarly experienced and skilled individuals. You must be able to differentiate to succeed.*

- *Know Your Prospect: Candidates who can speak the hiring company's language are more likely have more meaningful conversations than those who have done little or no research.*
- *Demonstrate ROI: Just as there is an opportunity cost in a sale, there is one in your selection as a candidate. This can be related to the value you will bring to your function and role or to the outcomes your focuses and initiatives will bring to your work.*
- *Being an Authentic and Valued Future Colleague: You want to show your cultural fit to the organization you wish to join through demonstration of your values, behaviors, and philosophies. In other words, you want to be your authentic self.*

CHAPTER 10

Fear and Inertia

Chapter Summary

- While you cannot simply overrule millennia of environmental evolution, you can train yourself to recognize what is holding you back and overcome your fears.
- Do not suffer "what ifs." They are far worse than rejection.
- Learn how to practically recognize, counter and challenge your inner demons by identifying your values and philosophies linked to the outcomes you most want for yourself.
- Once you have put your challenges through a more positive mindset, use them to inspire you to a state of readiness to perform.
- Take the leap and ensure that you find time to reflect on the support and kindness you find in others as you proactively head toward your better, brighter future.

Fear and Delay

Rejection is life. Being vulnerable in the dating world is to open yourself up for potential disappointment and rejection. If we can do it there because the prize is so great, surely, we owe it to ourselves to put ourselves out there for our careers and professional journeys also. Is the prize not worth it there too?

Fear and risk of rejection are real inhibitors that can threaten to hold you back. In an endeavor such as creating new opportunity by proactively opening doors, you should be mindful of what is happening in your brain and train yourself to both recognize and overcome barriers to your advancing your cause. Fears are universal, and you are not alone. To put yourself out there in any context is to be vulnerable, but taking that leap is essential, not only for your own self-development and growth, but also as a means to show you practically that provided you are well prepared, and have compiled a strong outreach, that actually no calamities will visit you. Quite the opposite, support and encouragement will be your just rewards.

The Brain Science

The brain science behind the fears that lead to delay and inertia involves complex neurological processes that are rooted in our evolutionary history and shaped by our experiences and perceptions of the world around us. Precisely because many of these elements are ingrained in us, we should make a conscious effort to understand what is happening, and the emotions our minds are communicating. This requires ongoing discipline. As practiced as you might become, fear, nerves, and calamitous mental projections of what could go wrong will never be fully eliminated. Understand these as constant companions and use them to ensure you prepare well, for at the end of the day they are there to ensure that you turn up to be your best.

Our bodies and minds are wired for survival, and this phenomenon is something we will come into conflict with across many aspects of our lives. Take public speaking, for example. Many of us have a fear of public speaking that is so pronounced, that when interviewed on the topic, many suggested that they would prefer death, rather than standing up to deliver a speech to a group of strangers or peers. Public speaking to colleagues is often the worst as you know these people, and, if you have any imposter syndrome, this is when it will come out to shine!

This is the same fear that may be delaying you in making that outreach to a prospective employer who is currently a stranger to you. These sensations and brain-delivered messages will never go away. In terms of public speaking, you are likely to always feel nervous and sickly before a big formal presentation, but this is something we can turn to our advantage by rewiring our thinking to focus on the fact that this is the body simply preparing us for peak performance.

Remember my opening story about the interview process I got myself into? Despite having done this many times and my being a salesperson by profession and therefore used to rejection, I still found myself delaying. Delaying and worrying that the ship might be sailing as I waited. Delaying because I would have to find and deliver a compelling outreach to a senior leader, with an imposing title, from an institution that I knew did not look for candidates from my background. An unknown. In the face of all my experience and knowledge, I found myself holding back while growing increasingly frustrated with my doing so.

What this comes down to is the fear of rejection. Why does your mind create scenarios of humiliation or rejection when contemplating public speaking, or not going over to speak to that attractive person, or when preventing me from writing to the target of my next interview process? The reason is that we are hardwired to fear rejection and social humiliation. In an endeavor that is about selling yourself to create opportunity for advancement, you must find ways to recognize the symptoms and reprogram your mind to help support your cause. Here is an overview of the brain functions at play:

- **"Lizard Brain":** This colloquial term typically refers to the most primitive parts of our brains, which are often associated with instinctual, survival-oriented behaviors. We can be fighting not only upbringing, learning, and culture, but literally ourselves when we promote ourselves or put ourselves into uncomfortable situations.
- **Amygdala:** Is a small almond-shaped structure deep within our brains, pivotal in processing emotions, including fear. A part of the "lizard brain" that encompasses several brain regions, when faced with the possibility of rejection, the amygdala can become activated, triggering the body's stress response and generating feelings of fear and anxiety, letting your mind run wild with imaginations of disaster, as it also plays a role in the formation of emotional memories.
- **Neurotransmitter Release:** The brain releases neurotransmitters such as dopamine, serotonin, and cortisol in response to social stimuli, including the prospect of rejection. Dopamine is associated with pleasure and reward, which can reinforce behaviors that are perceived to be safe and familiar, while serotonin is involved

in mood regulation and can influence feelings of social acceptance or rejection. Cortisol is known as a stress hormone and increases in response to perceived threats, which in turn triggers the body's fight-or-flight response.

- **Negative Bias:** Beware of your brain focusing on negative as opposed to positive experiences and stimuli. If you focus on the negative, you can more readily anticipate bad or disastrous outcomes, therefore avoiding situations that might result in rejection.
- **Neutral Pathways and Conditioning:** Over time, repeated experiences or perceived social threats can strengthen neural pathways associated with fear or avoidance behaviors. This conditioning can make it more difficult to overcome perceived threats, leading to procrastination, avoidance, or inertia.
- **Threat Assessment:** The brain is constantly surveilling to determine threats to our well-being. In the case of possible rejection or social humiliation, the brain can perceive this as a threat to our social status.
- **Social Learning**: Individuals may learn to avoid rejection through others' experiences or by internalizing societal or cultural norms and expectations related to acceptance and belonging.

Cultural background, upbringing, and even ancestry significantly shape behaviors, attitudes, and perceptions, often creating challenges in today's individualistic world. Collectivist values, risk aversion, modesty, and hierarchical social structures can all make it difficult for individuals to embrace self-promotion, take bold risks, or network confidently. Fear of failure or stigma can also deter deviation from established norms. While these challenges can be daunting, they can be overcome by adopting a growth mindset and viewing risk-taking as a learning opportunity. The key is to focus on the emotions and obstacles you, as an individual, are facing, to allow for active work to address them.

Practical Techniques for Positive Change

Changing a risk-averse mindset does require some rewiring. You must acknowledge that your current state is holding you back from committing to change. This involves a gradual exposure to risk and deliberate practice. Techniques to consider here might include:

- Cognitive Reframing: Your reasons are unique.
- Exposure Therapy: Doing more of what makes you feel uncomfortable.
- Developing a Growth Mindset and Open versus Fixed Thinking.
- Building Resilience to Rejection.

Consider the following strategies:

- **Recognize Fears:** The first step is to acknowledge your fear and understand the underlying reasons for your risk aversion. Identify past experiences, beliefs, or perceptions that have contributed to your current mindset. Self-reflection can help you to cast these drivers in a more positive light.
- **Challenge Negative Beliefs:** Question whether your fears are realistic or the result of exaggerated perceptions. Our minds can do a splendid job of imagining the worst of all outcomes. Consider, instead, alternative perspectives and evaluate the potential benefits of taking calculated risks.
- **Start Small:** Taking small, manageable risks to build confidence and familiarity with uncertainty can build confidence. Start with low-stakes decisions or scenarios where potential consequences are minimal and gradually increase the level of risk you perceive, until you are more comfortable with uncertainty. Role-play or practice can help to prepare you.
- **Set Realistic Goals:** Be specific about what you are trying to achieve as an outcome. I have spoken in the book about having the simple goal within a first-time meeting with a new contact, to just get to the next conversation. This is as far from an exaggerated outcome as you can get. There is no thought to landing a contract for employment at this stage. The diameter of focus is to interest the other party sufficiently to get to the next meeting. Focus on the process rather than the outcome. It could be that you want to test an assumption or practice a way of describing

your impact, approaches, and outcomes to a particular role. Take time to review and celebrate your progress along the way. Always absorb your learnings to better shape approaches and goals for the next time. Think in terms of "incremental gains," rather than transformative steps. Having a clear set of objectives helps you overcome reticence or fear.

- **Support and Guidance:** Learn how to ask for help. Identify and surround yourself with people who will encourage you or challenge you to step outside of your comfort zone. Accountability ensures that you will follow through. Also consider who in your network is expert in ways you perceive you are not. Simply ask them how they approach similar situations, what their process is, and how they would advise your next steps. You will be amazed how many battle the same demons as you do. This helps to diminish the challenge you feel, as you will discover that fears are universal and can be overcome. Remember to be specific in your ask of these people. You will be rewarded with a level of support you perhaps were not expecting.

- **Cultivate a Growth Mindset:** Emphasize learning, resilience, and embracing challenges as opportunities for growth. View setbacks or failures as valuable learning experiences rather than insurmountable obstacles or reasons to leave the path you are on. Focus on incremental gains, continuous improvement, and adaptability.

- **Practice Mindfulness:** Techniques such as deep breathing or visualization can help to manage anxiety and increase resilience in the face of uncertainty. It can also help to reinforce your capacity for self-awareness, regulate your emotions, and help you approach events and situations with clarity and calmness. Remember that feelings of nervousness are natural and are positive, as they are the body's mechanisms to prepare for performance. They ensure that you are operating in a peak way, so learn to embrace them, and use them to ensure you are present in every moment as you need to be. Always be kind to yourself. We can be our own worst critics. Sometimes the best way to overcome this is to gain feedback from others on your approach, how you came across, and what you might improve.

- **Celebrate Your Successes:** Many people who struggle in this area do not take the time to review and acknowledge great outcomes. Think in terms of, *"What went well? What went badly? What could I improve?"* Once you have captured these elements, recognize the achievement and courage it took to step outside of your comfort zone. Celebrating your successes will reinforce positive behaviors while building confidence. Having a sense of what you can improve will ensure you always think in terms of what incremental gains you can make.

Investigating Emotions

Do be conscious of any emotion, and especially any negativity, that you may be feeling. This could be nervousness, imposter syndrome, or simply a fear of the unknown. This is all entirely natural, but taking these negative emotions into your interview process is likely to make you view every moment through the lens of these. Start to isolate and address all these emotions or feelings early.

Identify and discern the reasons why you are feeling what you are feeling. You will need to be aware of these new inputs and the effects they may have in a way you never had to consider before. Ignoring and pushing on is not a recipe for helping to grow your candidacy. We can all be our own worst critics, so check on your confidence levels and, especially, how unkind you are being to yourself. Remember, the stories we tell ourselves are a way of programming the mind. Preparation and role-playing interview scenarios to yourself can also be a fabulous way to counter negative emotions and to help reprogram ourselves to break engrained, embedded neutral pathways and ways of thinking.

The practical way to begin to reset is to list what you are feeling, why that might be so, what these feelings are preventing you from achieving, and what outcomes you want for yourself. Jot these down without immediately trying to find solutions, do not ignore them and do consider putting them through a positive forward-thinking structured exercise. An example framework exercise to undertake at this point would be to ask yourself some open questions:

- What am I feeling? (Lack of confidence, concern about what I do not know, imposter syndrome, not knowing where to focus, fear of conflict, etc).
- What is the impact this emotion is having on me right now? (Why am I feeling this way toward this situation or person or perceived weakness?)
- What is the positive shift I would like to make right now and why?
- How will I address these feelings the next time they arise?
- What is the one thing I could change to improve my performance?

By thinking about and answering these questions, you are already putting anything negative you are feeling into a more positive light.

Another practical way to begin the process of breaking any negative emotions is to start with your values and understanding what got you here. An exercise to help you identify your values and candidacy abilities as part of defining your application is presented later. Once you have done this, focus on your vision, mission, and goals and start to lean into some positive, more confident thoughts.

Carving out time for yourself is to acknowledge that you, and what you are feeling, is important and is a vital component in building a better you. Embarking on personal and professional growth often involves deliberate placing of oneself into uncomfortable situations. This concept is rooted in the idea that stepping outside of one's comfort zone is fostering learning, resilience, and adaptability. Yes, investigating your emotions and fears might be uncomfortable, but consider them an opportunity to grow and enhance your appeal. When individuals purposefully expose themselves to challenges or unfamiliar territories, (including internal reflection), they confront new perspectives, skills, and experiences that contribute to their overall development.

Ultimately, the process of growing through discomfort is a deliberate and proactive approach to self-improvement. It's about recognizing that true growth often lies just beyond the boundaries of familiarity and complacency, encouraging individuals to embrace challenges as stepping stones toward becoming their best selves.

Figure 10.1 is a template that you can use to capture elements you are keen to isolate and unpack. The more precisely you define these, the more constructive your investigation into them can be.

Incremental Gains

Incremental or marginal gains refer to the process of making gradual and continuous improvements to performance, processes, or outcomes over time. These improvements are typically small in scale but, when accumulated, lead to significant overall progress and positive outcomes. When you are considering making a change to long-held behaviors or beliefs, the journey from here to there can seem daunting. By considering the changes or improvements you wish to make in smaller steps, the effort, and, by extension, the fear of making these steps is reduced.

A prominent example from the sporting world came from the world of cycling, through the efforts of Sir Dave Brailsford, a British cycling coach. His approach as performance director for British cycling was based on the idea that making small, incremental improvements in multiple aspects of cycling could lead to significant overall gains. Brailsford's approach yielded remarkable results. Under his leadership, British cycling achieved unprecedented success in the Olympics. Team Sky, whom he also represented, won multiple Tour de France titles. Initiatives and improvements do not need to be revolutionary or seismic to make a significant impact.

Incorporate and structure this approach into your journey and your self-reviews, and you will ignite and strengthen an approach centered around positive steps toward your goal. Changing a risk-averse mindset takes time, patience, and persistence. By taking gradual steps, challenging limiting beliefs, and seeking support when needed, you can gradually expand your comfort zone and embrace opportunities for growth and success.

All of this underscores the fact that one cannot easily defy what is ingrained or instinctual, such as responses governed by the amygdala

What Am I Feeling Right Now?

Answer:

(Clear, concise, truthful to yourself in the current moment; reflective of emotional state and concerns)

Emotion	Sensation	Reasons
Fear/Loss	I miss my colleagues and team, and I do not know what comes next. Anxiety, panic, anger	I am worried about money, and I do not know where to start on the search
Imposter Syndrome	I obsess about what I do not know. Inadequacy.	Is job less a proof point?
Lost	I feel my network is underdeveloped, who can I speak to? Overwhelmed and tired	Uncertainty is paralyzing me.

Desired outcomes and results

List: (Clear, measurable, time orientated)

1. Manage my emotions – I have practical fears and fear of rejection and judgment, I must focus on my accomplishments and update my CV and LinkedIn positively, then make a plan to progress into work sourcing conversations

2. Identify who to talk to – I need support, encouragement, and advice

Figure 10.1 Negative emotions template

and the "lizard brain." However, it's essential to recognize that these primal instincts may influence our behaviors and that conscious effort is often required to overcome them, especially when it comes to effectively promoting oneself.

Using Emotions to Inspire Preparation

Using negative emotions like nerves, anxiety, or even fear to prepare for a performance can be a powerful strategy when harnessed constructively. While these emotions are often viewed as obstacles, they can provide a valuable source of energy and focus. Many performers from athletes to musicians to public speakers use the adrenaline and the heightened awareness that comes with nervousness to sharpen their focus to prepare for peak performance. Rather than attempting to eliminate these feelings, they learn to channel them into positive outcomes.

One of the most helpful ways to reframe nerves is to recognize them as a sign of investment. Feeling nervous often means that the action you are about to undertake matters to you, which can be a powerful reminder of why you are putting in the effort. Acknowledging this can help transform nervousness from a dreaded sensation into a motivator. If a musician feels jittery before stepping on stage, that energy can be redirected into a more passionate and intense performance. Athletes often use "pre-game jitters" to achieve a state of heightened alertness, readying their minds and bodies to respond quickly under pressure.

Additionally, nerves and anxiety can serve as a source of mental preparation, allowing you to assess and plan for challenges. Visualizing potential scenarios, both positive and negative, can help build confidence and adaptability. For example, a speaker anticipating a question that might make them nervous can practice responding calmly, which both reduces uncertainty and builds resilience. This is also why role-playing an interview is a very useful exercise to get into. Just being practiced with your narratives can help to ease you when it comes to the time to perform.

These emotions can be a valuable source of data, highlighting areas that may need extra attention. By working through these scenarios mentally, candidates can create a sense of familiarity with potential obstacles, reducing the likelihood of being caught off guard. Remember though, that you cannot prepare for all questions or outcomes and that this is also good. Preparation enables you to be less focused on yourself and whatever you are feeling, such that the longer a conversation or interview goes on, the more comfortable and natural you feel. Accept that the other person will want to ask questions to get to a better sense of you, your motivations, or your processes. We will investigate ways to best handle unexpected questions later in Chapter 12: Enhanced Interview Preparation.

Remember the Mission

Changing the mindset and proactively engaging the job market to find your own opportunities does require a fundamental changing of the game, which may be an uncomfortable process for some. The phrase itself encapsulates the idea that by shifting one's perspective, attitude, and approach, one can affect significant transformations and outcomes.

The recruitment process is like a dance, you need to learn how to take the lead, guiding the process in a way that showcases your strengths and positions you well for the role. This approach starts from the moment you enter the process. By shifting your mindset to one of curiosity and resourcefulness and seeing setbacks as opportunities for growth-based learning, you can better adapt along the way. In the recruitment process, only one person can effect change. That is you and you alone. *"Change the mindset and change the game"* is a call to action and, therefore, a reminder that through shifting what may be our present negative mindset to one that embraces growth, possibility, and resilience, we can unlock our full potential and create a brighter future for ourselves and those around us.

You have nothing to lose and everything to gain. Consider the prize, a better career, a better life, more money, and more prospects for advancement. Understand that the delivery of these outcomes is better than any ill feeling toward reaching out to one person on that journey. You must, however, also develop a healthy sense of:

Hang on tightly. Let go lightly.

Which is to say, go into any interaction with sincerity and purpose, but if, for whatever reason you do not get the response you want, or the person does not wish to meet with you, or if you are passed over for the job or receive no feedback during a drawn-out process, then do not over think or obsess over what might have been. You gave it a fair shot. Nothing ventured, nothing gained. Reflect, move on, and try again. Resilience in this respect is key. Remember, you are waging a campaign to get where you want to be, not a set of individual battles. If you lose one skirmish it is not all for naught. The campaign can and will still be won in the end.

Takeaways

- *Take a proactive and positive approach to identifying and refocusing your fears.*
- *Understand your fears and the reasons behind inertia and use these to prepare yourself for performance.*
- *Always keep the end goal in mind.*
- *"Hang on tightly, let go lightly" and adapt and use all positive experiences and feedback as lessons to enhance your next approaches.*

CHAPTER 11

Dust off Your Best Stories and Your CV for Best Impact

Chapter Summary

- Ensure that you have identified and polished stories providing clear examples of achievement, overcoming challenges, and skills deployed in action.
- Have your values, behaviors, and philosophies on display and demonstrate these in the stories you tell.
- Consider your achievements beyond core competencies or role.
- If you have gaps in your CV, or if you are going for roles you are "overqualified" for, have your narrative primed as to your reasons and goals. Be clear about these upfront. Also, be more prepared to get around the HR and go direct.
- Be prepared to be "fluid," you never know where a conversation might take you, so encourage the free flow of ideas. Having your stories ready is part of taking control of the conversation.
- Be prepared to answer questions with questions if necessary and use the time to also interview the interviewer. Ensure you have good questions for them.

Never Let Your CV Do the Talking

One of the biggest misconceptions job candidates have when preparing for interviews is assuming that their CV will do the talking. The CV no doubt would have helped, but it really says little about you as a person.

Better to think that your CV is an essential tool for securing the interview, but that it's not enough to land the job.

Your CV is a static snapshot of your experience, qualifications, and skills, but it lacks depth. It will never be able to bring to life the capabilities and approaches you can bring to a role. It will not tell an interviewer how you will propose to go about the tasks and challenges ahead of you. Think in terms of leaving an interviewer with the most rounded sense of yourself and how you would apply yourself to the role. To be able to do that, you must probe and interview the interviewer, and that means a conversation must happen. This is why it's essential that your CV and your in-person performance are synchronized. To sell to maximum advantage, you need to be adept at bringing your value to life, and the best way to do this is through storytelling. Your CV should list your accomplishments within and beyond your core competence, and the processes and outcomes you can then demonstrate through storytelling. Stories are compelling, showing you in real-life scenarios. Consider always what the interviewer is likely to be looking for, whether essential skills, initiative, distilling information to priorities, actioning on focuses, planning, or sales, then make a list and think about your history in the context of how you might bring your relevant skills to life in the context of the role.

It staggers me frankly, how many times I have seen a CV and said to myself, "*I really want to meet this person*," only for someone else entirely to show up. I've always considered these candidates to have only done half of the job by not coming prepared on me and my company, by not coming with a sense of the role and how they would tackle it. Appearing for an interview without any kind of nuanced knowledge about the possible dynamics of the position or the company itself, to me, indicates a total lack of investment.

The Challenge with CVs

The issue with CVs in a transactional recruitment landscape is that you are putting your fate into the hands of someone who is not an expert in your industry and not an expert in handling and reviewing your type of profile and, hence, might not interpret your skills correctly. That's assuming your

CV gets through. If the screening algorithm has not thrown you out early, HR might not understand or recognize the companies you have worked for and their relevance to the role you are applying to. As generalists, they may not understand acronyms or industry jargon, so make sure you use long form and explain anything niche. Just because an HR is working for a company and in a market, do not expect them to understand that industry. The best do of course, but it is a function where many simply focus on the general duties of their role, they do not think about the specific needs of the business, unless they are very well briefed and managed by hiring managers. They will not be taking time to read your CV in detail, so ensure that you have a compelling description, list of skills and accomplishments, and that your keywords are on point. If you feel there might be any misinterpretation, ensure you deal with this upfront in summary sections or bullet points.

In a competitive recruitment landscape, recruiters will focus on the most likely to be accepted candidates, as such, they will often focus on those coming from competing companies. If your CV does not have the four or five companies that the hiring manager has mentioned, your CV will be summarily dismissed as the recruiter will favor those from the catchment pool most likely to result in a booking. For candidates expecting a fair process, this can feel unfair and disheartening, as it often puts them at a disadvantage from the start. It definitely means that the recruiter will not meet you to screen your skills. This is exactly the reason why we are focusing on bypassing the recruiter to get to hiring managers directly.

An interview will always be needed to corroborate and test for soft skills, but the extent to which a CV or an interview is used to make the final hiring decision can vary depending on the nature of the job, the industry, and the company's hiring practices.

Decided by CV

- **Technical Positions:** Requiring specific technical skills or certifications, such as software development, engineering, or data analysis. These rely heavily on the information provided in the CV to assess candidates' qualifications.

- **Academic or Research Positions:** Prioritizing candidates' educational background, publications, research experience, and academic achievements, which are typically detailed in the CV.
- **Highly Specialized Roles:** Requiring niche skills or expertise. These may place more emphasis on the CV to ensure candidates have the necessary qualifications and experience.

Decided by Interview

- **Soft Skills Evaluation:** Interviews are crucial for assessing candidate's soft skills such as communication, problem-solving ability, teamwork, adaptability, resilience, and leadership skills.
- **Cultural Fit:** Employers use interviews to evaluate candidate's compatibility with the company culture, values, and team dynamics. This involves assessing candidates' personality, work style, and alignment with the organization's mission.
- **Behavioral Assessment:** Interviews can often include behavioral questions that prompt candidates to provide examples of their past experiences to demonstrate their skills and judgment in action. This can better help assess a candidate's suitability for a role or environment.
- **Clarification:** Going beyond the CV to detail context about experiences, accomplishments, challenges, and career goals. The CV alone simply cannot convey this.

CV vs Networked Approaches

- **Networked:** You have had a conversation with someone in the hiring process, perhaps the person who will ultimately make the final decision. They will introduce you to HR and through HR will arrange the hiring panel. Your future boss will have briefed colleagues in terms of why you are a person who needs to be in the process. The CV is now a formality only.
- **Introduced by Headhunter:** A headhunter has contacted you based on your LinkedIn profile for a role they are managing. That first call is effectively your first interview, they are screening you

to make sure that you have the skills, experience, personality, and traits the hiring company needs. Once they have established that you are a candidate to put forward, then, your CV will be required. You are now already in consideration.

- **Response to Job Advert:** Here it is all on your CV and cover letter. Your CV is the very first, (and only), impression that you are making on this potential employer. The risk of immediate, summary rejection is high*.

"75 percent of resumes are rejected by an ATS before reaching a human Source" CNBC.com Kerri Anne Renzulli Article published February 28, 2019.

A CV Fit for Purpose

None of this is to say that your CV is unimportant. If you think of your CV as a calling card, then it is a first impression you are leaving on an organization, and how you enter the conversation matters. If you are leading with your CV in response to a job ad, your CV does all the talking initially but also consider how limiting this is. If you are leading with networking, the CV becomes just a formality that supports your candidacy as you're already guiding the conversation. Regardless of the approach, ensure that your CV is serving you well:

- **Market Yourself:** Strategically highlight your skills, achievements, and experiences. Demonstrate why you are the best fit for role.
- **Customize and Adapt:** Your CV is a tool. As you would for any job in the home, make sure the tool is right for the job you are applying it to. Lead with the qualities, skills, and achievements that best align to the role on offer. Study the job description and company language to gain as many clues as you can to increase your chances of success.
- **Showcase Your Value:** A CV can read like a dry list of companies, titles, and tenure. Add to this to showcase the value you would bring to an organization. By presenting your skills, accomplishments, and unique qualities effectively, you will demonstrate

the potential of your contribution to your future employer's goals and objectives.

- **Tee up Your Storytelling:** Make it easier for the person preparing to interview you to interview you well. In other words, trail the stories that will spark good conversations about how you would approach a role or what impact you would seek to deliver. A statement like, *"Doubled the business in under two years, by refreshing the go-to-market, focusing on winning value propositions, and changing the culture to support these outcomes,"* would lead to curious questions such as *"How did you achieve that?" "What practical steps did you take?" "What were your biggest challenges?"* and so on. The conversation is now yours, and this is what you want!

Why Stories Matter

If you are keen to move into middle-to-senior level roles, or any roles that come with a measure of managerial or leadership responsibility, even complex commercial roles, then you must be prepared to bring your stories. I say this because it is shocking to me how few interviewees seem to plan for interview with an eye toward differentiation.

I have over the years interviewed many candidates for roles, and, from my perspective as the interviewer, the CV is not what any interview is based on. The CV to me is all about sourcing, by which I mean shortlisting or defining who it is that you want to meet with. In that sense, the CV is table stakes, it gets you in the door, but it will never get you the job. At a bare minimum, your CV should be showing the experience and skills to potentially do the role along with highlighted key achievements. Only gaps or short tenures would interest me then. I would rarely base the interview on much more, unless stories were highlighted, because you want to know the person. Instead, I would want to look for:

- Cultural fit.
- Initiative and problem-solving capability.
- Prior success and understanding of the environment the person is potentially entering.

- A sense of philosophy or approach.
- A sense of the person's motivations, drivers, and values.

Key Elements of a Good Story

When you are in interview, it's about HOW you show up and how you might lead or transform a function. It's never about the WHAT. Hiring managers and recruiters don't just want to see what you have done on paper, they want to know *how* you did it and *how* you would go about the role on offer toward what outcomes. They are also evaluating whether you are the right fit for the team and the culture of the organization. When you are in an interview, telling stories that align with the company's values and the job's demands is the most effective way to prove a good fit in practice.

- **Provide Context**: A bullet point on your CV might say, "*Led a project that increased sales by 20%*." While impressive, it's a result without a story. In an interview, you can explain the obstacles you faced, how you identified the solution, and the leadership skills you demonstrated along the way. This gives depth to your accomplishments and makes them more memorable.
- **Showcase Your Behaviors and Values**: Companies are increasingly focused on hiring individuals whose values align with their own. By telling stories that highlight your core values, such as integrity, collaboration, or innovation, you can show not just what you've done but also how you approach challenges and contribute to a positive work environment.
- **Illustrate Your Problem-Solving Abilities**: Stories give you the opportunity to show how you handle real-world problems. In interviews, hiring managers often use behavioral questions like "*Tell me about a time when…*" to assess how you apply your skills under pressure. By preparing specific examples, you can clearly demonstrate your critical thinking, resilience, and decision-making process in ways that a CV alone never could.
- **Show Humility and Growth**: Your CV will often focus on your achievements, but interview stories are an excellent opportunity

to highlight moments where you faced challenges or failures and how you learned from them. These stories can humanize you, showing that you are open to growth and learning, which is a highly sought-after quality in candidates.

Remember as well, that if you are at the beginning of your career, that your stories can be adapted from life, sports, or studies, and used to address moments of learning and challenge, or to express where you would like to see your career go, or what you'd like to learn from an organization or leadership.

Every story you tell should follow a clear structure that gives the interviewer insight into not just the outcome but also your process. The **STAR method** is a tried-and-true approach for structuring your stories:

- **Situation**: Describe the context of the situation, giving the interviewer an understanding of the challenge or opportunity you were facing.
- **Task**: Explain your role in the situation and your responsibilities.
- **Action**: Detail the specific steps you took to address the problem or meet the challenge. Focus on your behaviors, decisions, and the skills you used.
- **Result**: Share the outcome of your efforts, quantifying your success if possible, and any reflections.

In addition, when you come to **Result**, it might be good to add **Emotion** and **Learning** to show your fully rounded takeaways from the situation you are describing. By using this method, you ensure that your stories are alive and informative. They give a full picture of how you operate in a professional setting and illustrate the value you can bring to the company.

Aligning Stories to Job Description and Company Culture

It's not enough to have a few pre-prepared stories, you need to ensure that the stories you tell are aligned with the specific job and the company's culture. Each interview will be different, and your approach should be tailored accordingly. To do this effectively:

- **Study the Job Description**: Before your interview, carefully analyze the job description. Identify the key skills, behaviors, and experiences that the company is looking for. Are they focused on leadership, problem-solving, or technical expertise? For example, if the job emphasizes collaboration, choose a story where you worked successfully in a team environment.
- **Research Company Values**: Most organizations publicize their core values on their website or in press releases. Are they focused on innovation? Do they emphasize customer service or community involvement? By understanding their values, you can select stories that highlight how your personal and professional philosophy aligns with theirs. If a company values sustainability, for instance, you might share a story about how you implemented environmentally friendly practices in a previous role.
- **Focus on Transferable Skills**: Sometimes, your experience might not perfectly align with the job you are applying for. Telling stories that focus on transferable skills, such as communication, leadership, adaptability, and time management, can bridge the gap. These stories show that you can bring relevant, adaptable skills to new challenges, even if the exact role is new to you.

Stories Can Shape Your Interview Strategy

Relying solely on your CV to speak for you in an interview is a passive approach. Interviews are your chance to show not just what you have done but also who you are and how you work. By coming prepared with stories, you can:

- **Take Control of the Narrative**: Rather than waiting for the interviewer to ask about a particular skill or experience, your stories give you a way to proactively steer the conversation toward your strengths. If the interviewer asks about a general skill, like leadership or teamwork, you can pivot to a prepared story that highlights your most relevant and impressive experience.

- **Showcase a Broader Range of Skills**: In person you can expand on contributions beyond your core focus, such as volunteer work, side projects, or personal experiences that shaped your professional behavior or philosophy.

- Be **Prepared for Difficult Questions**: Interview questions, such as "*What is your greatest weakness?*" or "*Tell me about a time you failed,*" can be challenging if you are not prepared. However, having a story ready where you discuss how you learned from a failure or addressed a weakness, turns these questions into opportunities to show growth and resilience. It also allows you to demonstrate emotional intelligence, an increasingly valued trait in candidates.

- **Create Emotional Connection**: Data and bullet points are important, but stories resonate on a deeper, emotional level. They allow you to connect with the interviewer, making you more memorable. A well-told story that showcases your passion, dedication, and enthusiasm for your work will linger in the interviewer's mind long after the interview ends.

Takeaways

- *Think of your CV as what will get you in the door. All versions should reflect you as best they can. Add your stories in summary into the achievements at a high level.*
- *Think about fine-tuning your CV for each specific opportunity.*
- *In interview, your CV no longer does the talking. You do.*
- *It is astounding how many candidates come without the stories of their life or career prepared. Do not be like these candidates. Get your stories lined up to demonstrate your strengths, values, and approaches to work challenges.*
- *Focus your stories on soft skills, communication, collaboration, problem-solving, initiative, creativity, and teambuilding.*

Competence and experience may get you in the door, but soft skills win you the role.

- *Even blank spots in the CV or multiple moves can be bettered, provided that your story shows a through line. Have a narrative for what has brought you to the interview today and where you hope to be in 3 to 5 years' time.*

CHAPTER 12

Enhanced Interview Preparation

Chapter Summary

- *Prepare well for any interview to guarantee that you are ready and on point when most needed. There is no substitute for good preparation. Be practiced speaking about your experience and expertise, especially if interviews are coming few and far between. There is nothing worse than feeling undercooked.*
- *Where are you getting your information from? Concentrate on creating quality conversations geared to fully understanding the culture and role as well as how you will affect an impact.*
- *Use every chance to differentiate; it is staggering how little research candidates do when preparing for interview.*
- *Do not rely solely on company website research. Websites can be easily misinterpreted, especially if the role on offer is for a specific commercial operation or entity, for example.*
- *Broaden your inputs; LinkedIn, web, articles, posts, socials, YouTube, presentations, network, and direct hiring panel outreach.*
- *Use techniques to handle unexpected questions.*

By failing to prepare, you are preparing to fail.

Benjamin Franklin

"What is an interview to you?" If you think of interviews as simply a process of a hiring company looking at and asking questions of you, then you are missing everything. Once you have gained an opportunity to sit in front of a hiring panel, you should be thinking in terms of:

- **Interviewing the Company:** Learning about the role, the culture, the expectations, the measures of success, the potential to work or grow beyond your core focus, the environment, opportunities for travel, the philosophy and leadership style of the company and of your immediate boss.
- **Test Assumptions:** Test your research and demonstrate that you have taken the time to think in-depth about your approach and impact in the role on offer in the context of what the company is facing, from challenges to opportunities.
- **Positioning Yourself Proactively:** Everything should be focused on demonstrating how you, and your approach to role, will differentiate. If you are in sales, this means a one-pager on where you will focus, how you will win, what support you will need, and what you anticipate delivering in the first year, for example. Remember, this does not have to be delivered in the first round of interview, but throughout the process, and particularly if you feel that the process is "drifting."

Doing Your Research

Based upon my experience of interviewing folks for roles, I know that few do adequate research with a view to providing a platform for deeper interview conversations. I suspect this is mostly due to a fear of being off the mark, but consider the benefits in terms of differentiation from other candidates. Consider that developing fact-based conversations about the actions you would take in the business is really a springboard to an effective start to your time in role.

So many times, in interview, the candidate will base insights on the company website alone, which can often be misinterpreted. Such "research" is never enough, it is also quite lazy. You must be ready for questions like; "*What do you know of our company?*" or "*What is your sense of the role on offer?"* I would always ask these questions to have a sense of how the individual has applied themselves to the job of understanding the role on offer and how they might bring themselves to it. The danger of relying on basic website research is that you can rarely know a company fully unless you are in it. A company may have multiple divisions and multiple offerings, you cannot assume that your role is working across them all. You must build a better level of knowledge of the environment you are interviewing for. I always prefer a candidate who has shown the initiative to dig deeper and present themselves in a differentiated manner than those who do nothing or just the bare minimum. If uncertain, say so. Explain your process and interpretation as this is a two-way conversation and the other side will guide you.

Interview preparation goes far beyond simply showing care and commitment. It's about steering the conversation in a way that deepens your understanding and advances your candidacy. Failing to research beforehand risks leaving you exposed and reactive, relying solely on the interviewer's interpretation of your potential. Without preparation, you surrender control and with it, the opportunity to shape how your skills, character, and value are perceived.

How to flesh out your research and look for clues? Consider the following:

- The Job Advert.
- The Corporate Website.
- The Annual Report.
- Company Blogs.
- Hiring Manager Interviews.
- LinkedIn, Twitter (X), Facebook.
- Competitor Corporate Websites.
- Corporate News.
- Corporate Presentations (SlideShare).
- Product or Service Comparison Websites.
- Glassdoor Employee Reviews.
- Gartner "Magic Quadrant."
- Investment Sites, such As "Motely Fool."

This I am sure is not an extensive list and you may well have discovered assets or favorite places to discover information. I'd love to hear about these if you have. Let's investigate some of these in a little more detail.

The Job Advert

As discussed, there are really two types of job posting, the External Recruiter Job Advert and the Direct Hiring Company Job Posting. The former are tricky as the recruiter is deliberately suppressing information as it is not in their interests to expose too much . The second of these, the Direct Hiring Company Job Postings, are great as they usually go into more detail. Topics usually covered in these postings can be:

- Company High-Level Overview.
- Product Information at High Level.
- Reporting Line.
- Job Function Details.
- Required Candidate Experience.
- Required Candidate Skills.
- Soft Skills Required by the Candidate.
- Cultural Clues.
- Corporate Ambitions.

Carefully read these adverts and notice the clues and the language used. All of this is likely to be summary level at best, but you can use these highlights to narrow the focus on your research and chase down what is happening at the company in question.

The Corporate Website

A rich resource indeed. Here you will find much information organized neatly for you to absorb:

- Product or Service Focused Materials.
- Details on the Leadership.

- Details on the Corporate Mission, Values, and Corporate Story to Date.
- The Annual Report and Other Presentations.
- Case Studies and Testimonials.

Corporate Mission and Values

The first step I would advise would be to discover and note the Corporate Mission Statement and Values. This will give you a sense of the core values and passions of the organization. You will want to mirror the language in your CV, cover letter, and correspondence. You can also shape your stories to highlight similar attributes and values in action.

Once you have this, you can head to other resources to corroborate whether the company is living up to these published aspirations. Glassdoor, the annual report, and indeed anyone in your network who has either worked at, or who is working at the company in question, should be able to give you an insight as to whether the company is as true as its word.

Competitive Reviews

How likely are you to go and buy a product without researching reviews and alternatives? Why would you not do the same for the company you are intending to interview for? Once you have reviewed your prospective company's offerings, go and check out their competition. Google searches and Gartner Magic Quadrant searches may also give you a sense of where your prospect company stands in the market. Even if you are not in a commercial role, it is important that you understand what the company does and why it differentiates. If you can tie that back to the mission, you can articulate how your contribution in your area or function will support the overall goals for the business.

Company History

Understand the corporate journey and their current position and focuses within their industry, their technology, and future growth journey. Use the annual report executive statements and even investment sites such as "The Motley Fool," to understand how the company is performing in the market, (provided the company is listed), what their financials tell you, and what challenges they may be facing.

The Annual Report

There is so much useful information in a company's annual report. You will find these and other statements and presentations in the "Investor Relations" part of the corporate website. The Annual Report is the report card that the company must issue to the investment community every year. It looks back over the past year's trading performance and forward to the next year.

The report will openly cover successes, challenges, and the competitive environments faced by the management team. You will also discover the focuses and plans the company is concentrating on for the next year. Of course, there is also the Profit and Loss statement and accounts that can be useful to understand. You want to get a sense of how the business is traveling financially, whether it is profitable, whether its revenue has increased over the last 5 years, which segments are growing, and so on. You do not have to be an investor or a financial guru to understand these reports, so please do not be intimidated by them. Areas that you should concentrate on are:

- **The Annual Report Introduction**: A good place to get a summary sense of the direction of travel for the business.
- **The CEO or MD's Statement**: Usually, there will be a commentary on the previous trading period, as well as an articulation of any challenges or focuses the company is facing going forward. Use this to question how your role rolls up to the overall performance and outcomes of the business while tying your contributions toward these as well.
- **The Finance Director's Statement**: Similar to the above, and full of insightful business commentary, this is a useful resource to see where the focuses and challenges may lie. There could be mention of costs, efficiencies, and other indications that will help you

ascertain where you can shape your effectiveness to help support the focuses of the business.

- **The HR Director's Statement**: Keep an eye out for cultural and people content here and use this to highlight your cultural fit through your values and behaviors in action.

Company Blog

Increasingly you will find corporate blogs as part of a company's Content Marketing Strategy. Check whether your Hiring Manager has ever posted, and get a sense of where they see focuses and competition. The blog will also give a sense of how the company positions its products or services.

Hiring Manager Research

In earlier chapters, I outlined how you can easily find the Hiring Manager's digital footprint in terms of articles, posts, comments, and corporate video content. Ensure that you search on Google to see if they have written about, been interviewed, or posted any material that may be helpful. Interviews or articles are usually fantastic resources to find. Use a simple search such as:

"TargetPersonName + TargetPersonJobTitle + CorporateName + Interview + Article + Blog"

LinkedIn, Twitter (X), and Facebook

A simple visit to your Hiring Manager's LinkedIn, Twitter (X), and Facebook profiles will tell you much.

- Are you already connected to them and by whom?
  - A great icebreaker is to discuss connections you have in common.
    - These connections might also offer insight into the person before you write to them or meet with them.

- Their job history:
  - ○ Do you have any connectivity or topics you can discuss as a result?
- Recommendations or endorsements on the profile:
  - ○ These could give you an insight to the person's qualities, skills, and passions.
  - ○ Could offer clues on their leadership style.
- Engagement activity:
  - ○ Have they posted or written any articles?
  - ○ Discover what posts they have engaged with.
  - ○ What are their passions or points of view.
- Personal blogs, Twitter (X), and other social networking websites:
  - ○ What are their personal interests?
  - ○ Do you share support for any sports teams?
  - ○ Do you share hobbies?
    - ▪ All of the above is fuel for great icebreakers.

Competitor Websites

It is often informative to see how competitors represent their product and services. Do they do a better or worse job and why? What topics do they focus on regarding their content marketing? If you have time, you may want to read the competitors' annual reports as well. This step is better for the second interview and beyond or if you are making recommendations in your 90-day plan or other presentations you send as part of "Breaking the Recruitment Process." If you do not know who the competition is, you can undertake a simple Google search such as:

"TargetCorporateName + Competition + Reviews"

There are many industry, or software specific comparison sites on the internet. Some will allow you to directly review a product or service against a selected competitor. These sites will also often contain customer reviews, which are also great to give you a sense of how the product is received in the marketplace. Be careful though, some sites will not fully understand a product or service and may not categorize against competitors on a truly "like for like" basis. Still, this is a great question to raise at interview, for example, if there are bad reviews, or to ask whether a site has correctly identified and grouped the company's products.

A quick word of caution regarding reviews. Happy users or customers do not always endorse or review products or services, particularly if they are simply "content." Unhappy or angry customers will "shout loudest." That said, you may well find out issues or complaints that will inform you prior to interview in terms of questions you may be able to ask. Similarly, when using Glassdoor, unhappy ex-employees will criticize more freely. If there are a number of and a consistency to complaints, there could, however, be something to it.

Corporate News

This is a very quick and easy search you can make to see what news is trending right now about a target company. This is typically feedback from the investment community. If they are optimistic or pessimistic about a company, it is important to understand the reasons behind their view. Simple put the company name, perhaps their stock market ticker as well, into Google and hit "News."

Presentations (SlideShare)

SlideShare is owned by LinkedIn and is an incredible resource for those wanting to learn about companies. It is also a great resource when making your 90-day plan or other presentations as part of the recruitment process because you can use the templates for your documents. By doing this, you are subtly aligning your documents to the company's, as if you are already working for them. (We will cover this topic in Chapter 13: Shaping the Interview Process and Post-Interview Strategies). There are three ways to go about finding target company presentations:

1. Enter a search on Google, for example, "CorporateName + .ppt."
2. Go to SlideShare, sign up, (this allows you to download presentations,) and search directly on the site.
3. Check the Investor Relations page.

Beware that on SlideShare, the .ppt templates, logos, and corporate colors may well be out of date, so check on the corporate website if you are taking anything as a presentation template for second or third interviews.

Glassdoor Reviews

Glassdoor can give you a sense of what it is like in a company. You will find information on the interview process, the management and employee reviews past and present. As mentioned, the angry will be more vocal. That said, there could be trends or topics you can uncover that could inform your approach. It is perfectly acceptable to bring up perceptions about leadership if the feedback is consistent. It is also perfectly reasonable to ask consistent questions to all in the interviewing panel, not everyone is self-aware or open to feedback after all, so getting multiple perspectives on the culture, leadership style, support networks, and so on is vital for you the candidate in interviewing the company. It is a two-way process after all, and the company you are interviewing with should also be selling to you.

Gartner "Magic Quadrant"

Gartner Magic Quadrant provides comparison and commentary on several industries by rating competitor companies within their "Magic Quadrant." This is a commentary on the scope, vision and execution of corporate strategy compared to other players. Reports are usually fee based, however, you can often find the reports for free, or at least the imagery, so you can see the ranking of your prospect company compared to others. If a company is proud of their Gartner placement, they will often provide links to the free report directly from the Corporate Webpage. All you have to do is sign up and download. Alternatively, you can use searches and image searches on Google like this:

"TargetCorporateName + Gartner Magic Quadrant"

If you then search for "Images," you can often find the magic quadrant itself. The full report, if you can get it, is useful as each company is covered in some detail, which can provide you with a great deal of information. Be conscious that Gartner is an outside agency commentating on industries, hence, it is quite possible that they may incorrectly categorize or understand a product or offering. Even so, this still offers you the opportunity to ask great questions or position statements effectively in interview.

A Hunter Mentality

Treat research like a game. You are the detective, searching out the information that will provide you with compelling approaches to the hiring manager. Remember all the while you are doing this, you are in effect preparing for interview. You will be so much more confident and at ease having researched and developed your understanding.

Reaching Out to the Interview Panel, Ex-employees, or Connections

Do not be afraid to do this. Use LinkedIn to find folks you are connected to who have either worked at the company in question or with the hiring manager. Be open and ask for a quick call or meeting so that you might prepare to get a better sense of the landscape before the interview. Simply say you are preparing for an interview, (mention the role and other details), and would value a short catch-up to ask about the company, their focuses, challenges, their culture, and the leadership style. Ask for any other pointers that might help you to be successful as well.

Handling Unexpected Questions

Handling unexpected questions in interview can feel challenging, but with the right techniques, you can respond thoughtfully even when caught off guard. The first thing I would advise is that you go into any face-to-face interaction alive to the fact that any question could be fired at you. Simply being in the moment and well-practiced on your stories will prepare you to strongly handle questions in the moment. Here are some strategies to help you think on your feet and deliver under pressure:

- **Pause and Breathe:** Taking a pause, even for a second or two, can help you avoid blurting out an unstructured answer. This brief pause can also convey confidence and thoughtfulness.
- **Acknowledge the Question:** If the question is surprising, compose yourself by saying, "*That's an interesting question*," or "*I hadn't thought of that before*," demonstrating to the interviewer that you are carefully considering the question while giving yourself time to approach the topic thoughtfully.
- **Break Down the Question:** For complex or layered questions, break it down into manageable parts. Address one part at a time or rephrase the question in your mind (or aloud), to ensure you understand it fully before answering. If you are not sure of an answer, you can share part of your thought process to show how you are approaching the problem. This can be especially useful for hypothetical questions or problem-solving scenarios, as it reveals your analytical skills.
- **Frameworks to Structure Your Answer:** Applying a simple structure can bring clarity to your answer. Here are a few that work well in interviews:
  - **STAR Method:** For behavioral questions, use Situation, Task, Action, Result, to structure an answer that illustrates your experience.
  - **Problem-Solution-Result:** Describe a problem, the solution you would consider, and the positive result or impact you would aim for.
  - **Pros and Cons:** When asked for your opinion or judgment on a topic, briefly outline pros and cons before stating your conclusion.
- **Reflect on Past Experiences**: Draw on your experience, even if it doesn't seem directly related to the question. Saying something like "*In a similar situation, I handled it by…*" shows your adaptability and creativity in applying your skills to new contexts.

- **Admit When You Don't Know (and Pivot)**: If you are truly stumped, it's better to acknowledge it gracefully than to stumble through. You can say something like "*I'm not certain, but here's how I would approach finding the answer...*" This shows humility, resourcefulness, and a problem-solving mindset. For open-ended or speculative questions, show how you would approach the unknown rather than trying to perfectly answer. For example, "*If I encountered this scenario, I'd start by gathering information on...*" or "*I'd evaluate it by looking at X, Y, and Z.*"
- **Stay Positive and Confident**: Keep your tone positive avoiding self-doubting phrases like "*I'm not sure if this is right.*" Speaking confidently, even if you are unsure, gives a better impression and shows resilience under pressure.
- **Circle Back If Necessary**: If you think of additional points later on, reflect back, "*Actually, I'd like to add...*" This shows thoughtfulness and ensures your best points make it into your answer.

Using these techniques, you can turn even the most unexpected questions into opportunities to demonstrate your critical thinking, adaptability, and poise. With practice, handling "curveball" questions can become a strength.

The Power of Silence. For the Interviewer

A word on silence. Silence is the salesperson's greatest asset, and also that of the interviewer, but few can honestly use it well. A great salesperson or interviewer will ask a challenging open-ended question and then they will simply shut up, letting that silence become tangible, not letting the other person off the hook. This is often when the most candid responses are elicited. The other person in the conversation feels compelled to fill the void and usually with honest, not always structured responses, which can be quite revealing. But this is a skill. I have witnessed countless times when a killer question has been asked, and the person asking cannot themselves handle the silence, which they then rush to fill, always with a softball, easier question, thereby letting the other side off the hook. Being on the other side of this is something you must prepare for in interview.

The danger comes when you are asked a great question and the silence is maintained. Be confident and do not be afraid to ask the interviewer to repeat the question or to answer that question with a question of your own, to focus on what exactly the person wants to learn or know. Also be prepared to use this technique on your interviewer, particularly if asking challenging questions.

The Fear of Inaccuracy

Once you have completed your research, be confident in the fact that you will not know all things at this stage, as someone looking into a business from the outside. If you can substantiate or test assumptions by reaching out to connections on LinkedIn, then so much the better, but 100 percent accuracy is not the aim here.

Remember, no one will know a company as intimately as the people working at that company. It is ok to get things wrong but know this, the hiring manager will see your initiative, your passion and will appreciate that you have gone to such lengths to prepare. By doing so, you have increased the chance that they will coach you toward next steps or meetings. The work now, is to take all this information and shape it into approaches that will not only support your interview journey but, more importantly, will get you that job!

Role-play

When I have an interview, in fact if I am preparing for a podcast or key-note, I always practice my lines. What I am really practicing here is my delivery and language, while ensuring that the stories I am relating about my experience land well. Doing this ensures that when you are in the situation, you are already more confident about your language, messages, and delivery. You can then set about handling your emotions, questions, and the environment better.

Limiting Negative Self-Language

You may think you are being humble or self-depreciating. You may think that you are limiting the potential of sounding boastful or, as discussed earlier, you may be addressing your relationship toward self-promotion. However, you should consider what you could be doing if you are unintentionally using language that could be harmful to how you are perceived by others. Limiting language often reflects self-doubt, insecurity, or a lack of confidence in one's abilities. In truth, it can hold you back from opportunities and diminish how others perceive you. Here are some examples of limiting language when discussing oneself:

- **"I'm only…" or "I'm just…"** Example: *"I'm just an assistant"* or *"I'm only doing my job."* This minimizes your role and contributions, implying you don't see your value. Focus on your achievements and the challenges you have overcome.
- **"I've only been doing this for…"** Example: *"I've only been in this field for two years."* This minimizes your experience and implies you are less capable. Focus instead on the initiatives and positive impacts you have made.
- **"I don't have much experience in…"** Example: *"I don't have much experience in leadership, but…"* This not only undermines your qualifications but also sets the bar on your perceived readiness to accept responsibility and sets an overall negative tone before even presenting your strengths.
- **"I guess I'm okay at…"** Example: *"I guess I'm okay at managing projects."* This shows uncertainty and lack of confidence in your abilities.
- **"I'm not really an expert in…"** Example: *"I'm not really an expert in marketing, but I've done some work in that area."* This downplays your skills, even if you have relevant experience or knowledge.
- **"I was lucky to get the role…"** Example: *"I was lucky to get the promotion."* This suggests your success is due to luck, rather than your qualifications or hard work. Focus instead on how you have made the role your own and your achievements in the position.
- **"I hope I can manage…"** Example: *"I hope I can manage this project."* This language suggests uncertainty and a lack of confidence in your capability to handle tasks.

- **"I'll try…"** Example: *"I'll try to complete this task."* "Try" sounds less committed and less confident compared to saying, *"I will complete this task."*
- **"It's not a big deal…"** Example: *"I led the project, but it's not a big deal."* This diminishes the significance of your achievements and contributions.
- **"I'm not good at…"** Example: *"I'm not good at presentations, but I'll give it a shot."* Starting with a negative self-assessment weakens the listener's confidence in your abilities.

Understand that it is good to be honest. I recall an interview for a role within an industry I had only been on the periphery of previously.

The executive vice president (EVP) interviewing me began by explaining their business. My inexperience in the industry troubled me, and I raised my hand to point out that while I totally understood the environment and solutions being discussed, I did not have direct experience of the space. The immediate response was *"It does not matter."* I knew straightaway that something else was at stake here. As the EVP continued, I thought to myself *"Why am I sitting here?"* and I concluded that it must be my experiences of building sales teams and cultures married to my enterprise and start-up experiences. This indeed turned out to be true. As I continued my interview process, meeting other senior leaders on the interview panel, I began to flesh out a picture of a business unit that had lost its way. This also allowed me to be more confident about why I was there, especially when later I was managing some difficult personalities as part of executing a turnaround and establishing a cultural reset to the region in question.

I tell this story as limiting language would have ended this opportunity for me. Instead, I expressed a concern with a *"but."* *"I want to point out that I have only been on the periphery of your industry, but I understand exactly where you are coming from…"* Already here, I have framed the conversation in terms of my transferable skills, perspectives, and approaches. As it turned out in this case, I was entering a "turnaround" situation that was one of the most rewarding experiences of my career to date.

Do learn the lesson of avoiding any types of negative or limiting language so that you might allow yourself to present with more confidence and assertiveness, helping others to recognize your value and potential contribution.

Takeaways

- *More research is better than less. Expand the sources for your information gathering.*
- *Being researched will increase confidence and will help you maximize any networked meeting you may curate or any interview you may attend.*
- *Be alive and present in any conversation so that you can handle curveball questions well.*
- *Use the data and perspectives you have gathered to direct questions and test assumptions, so you are consistently learning more about the environment, the leadership, the role, the focuses, and goals for the business.*
- *Make sure to position yourself, along with your skills, experiences, and achievements, at the core of the data you research. This way, you can effectively highlight your stories to uplift your candidacy and potential impact in the most compelling way possible.*
- *Be conscious of the language you are using to describe yourself.*
- *Role-play to help polish your narratives and ensure that your language is positively focused on your approaches, achievements, and outcomes.*
- *Start to gather your found and learned datapoints into actionable formats. Start to think in terms of one-pagers such as 90-day plans or in-role focus documents.*

CHAPTER 13

Shaping the Interview Process and Post-Interview Strategies

> ### Chapter Summary
>
> - The selection process does not end with the interview, far from it. Make sure you keep yourself in the spotlight.
> - If you are not already using 90-day plans or one-pagers for interview and within your job, consider them as a means of differentiation.
> - Bring your research to a conversational pivot whereby you start to shape and take control of the interview process.
> - Use tools that can display your values, focuses, and approaches, enabling you to change the conversation and drive toward a job offer.

Taking Control of the Interview Process

Don't just drift with the current. Grab the oars, chart your course, and steer toward the destination you desire.

Once you are in a recruitment process, it's all too easy to passively go through the motions of attending each conversation, perhaps sending thank-you emails afterward, and then waiting for the next update. This is all a choice, and you may well feel it is the way to behave as a candidate. If you are on the "inside" of the recruitment process, having taken all the steps outlined earlier in the book, then maybe this is indeed a viable course of action. The job interview process that brought me to Singapore from the UK, with a change of industry and an opportunity to manage a larger team across multiple countries was a bit like this, but then I was secure in the process, and I already knew that I was the shortlisted candidate behind the public job advert.

I had sold an IT solution to one of the world's largest logistics firms in Europe. It was a phenomenal success and was being rolled out country by country. We then white-labeled the solution to one of their business units, and they used me to resell this solution to their clients. I represented them in Europe to close several deals together, and I was then asked to come to APAC to support training and identification of opportunities within the region. As a result, I made my first Asia road trip, taking in Singapore, Hong Kong, and Shanghai. It was on my second trip that I was asked if I was interested to manage their sales team in APAC. I jumped at the chance. Even then the process took a long time, several months in fact, often with no feedback. I recall wondering many times what the latest news was. I know better now, of course, having lived and worked in Singapore for over 12 years, that the process of hiring a foreigner is complex, as the hiring company needs to clear various processes before being able to officially offer a contract for hire. This includes publicly posting the role and interviewing.

I was keen to start my new adventure, moving to a new country and I was keen to get stuck into my new role, but it was all taking time. Even so, I was comfortable within the process. My interviews had long since finished, and it was now just a waiting game. I was anxious, but secure in the knowledge this would all work out. I tell this story to prove a point. This was a brand-new industry for me. Therefore, do you think I'd have stood any kind of chance had I applied to an advertised role with my experience and CV? The answer is a resolute no. Being on the inside, I knew my prospective boss, and the company had a sense of me and I of them. This was the connected job market in motion. I was aligned with the hiring manager in terms of what he was looking for, we also shared approaches and philosophies on sales and selling. I understood their challenges, I was well briefed on the executive team, and I knew my application was unique. I was being hired as an outsider with specific sales leadership skillsets that the company perceived that they needed. This was a secure process.

Speeding Up Decisions

The fact of the matter is that sometimes you need to help the side recruiting to be able to make their mind up. Another time, I had recently become redundant and needed to find work in a hurry. This was post-pandemic Singapore, and employment passes (EPs) were, if anything, being canceled. It was also a very weak jobs market. I immediately went to my network, and a coffee meeting presented me with an introduction to a fast-growing payments company. I was getting easy access to the leadership, they were coming back to me and scheduling calls, but frankly, I felt like the process was drifting. I was on the clock with my life in Singapore in jeopardy if I had to leave and come back with no EP. I therefore had to change the dynamic. I decided to get proactive and force the issue. I used an approach I have developed over many interview processes, one essential to operating within the connected job market, one guaranteed to help you differentiate and, on most occasions, swing the process resolutely into your favor.

What I did, and what I would advise anyone to do, was to proactively and practically take the initiative to show how I would impact the role and, therefore, the hiring company directly. Almost every time I have done this, it has changed both the nature and the urgency of the interview processes. On this occasion, we shifted from what could be best described as "interested catch-ups" to a job offer overnight. The issue we are confronting in these circumstances, is that the hiring company still cannot quite commit as they need to understand the impact that can be made more clearly. The way to change this dynamic is to create a document that becomes the focus of the conversation. These tools are the "Directional One-Pager," and the 90-day plan, and this is how they work:

- Enable you to organize your thoughts, impressions, and data.
- Allow you to take control of the hiring process and table the practical topics that will lead to a contract for hire.
- Communicate something of one's method and approach.
- Create specific, actionable, and measurable plans tied to the mission.

- Depressurize yourself by bringing clarity to the challenges ahead.
- Ensure that you will be well-coached, supported, and aligned to your future hiring manager.

If you are not already using these documents within hiring processes, I would recommend you start doing so. Using approaches like these not only provides the hiring company with a structured approach that details something about your processes, philosophy, and personality, but allows you to test out ideas and perceptions that you may have coming into a business. It allows you to craft a deeper conversation in interview as you will raise substantive, impactful topics, and ideas for approaches. They allow you to take control and shape a dialogue around what you will bring.

Gather and Shape Your Insights

It is more than likely that you have a panel of discussions lined up, on average 3 to 5, sometimes more. For some of the largest companies, I've heard of up to 15 rounds of interviews, which seems excessive and counterproductive. That's a lot of perspectives on a role if you are attuned to ask great questions and listen. What you need to do now is to demonstrate what you have learned about the opportunity in front of you and to then apply your values and process to actively show the hiring company how you will go about the role, and with what anticipated outcomes and deliverables, aligned to the overall mission or goals of the business. You do not have to be 100 percent accurate at this point, and a solid approach here will help you to be coached toward the right emphases on topics. Taking this approach will help you to dictate your terms, provided you successfully execute, through always having a focus on your ROI, no matter what role you are applying to.

Interview Stage Analysis

Begin by reviewing your impressions of the recruitment process so far.

Use the template below, (Figure 13.1) to analyze your thoughts, takeaways, and feelings. Take some time to review these points and any others that might come to mind by jotting down your immediate reactions in

Define the company's challenges	• Inefficiencies, growth, culture, etc.
What is the impact I can make on the business?	• Describe the opportunity loss or cost to the client in not hiring you
What is my value proposition? How can I support the culture?	• Describe the return on investment for the client. What is my ROI through delivered objectives?
Impressions, what do I know? What do I need to ask?	• Does the company/role feel right to me?

Once you have identified the value you can bring, then broaden out the research to make the most compelling case for hire

Who can I reach out to for help? Do I have network who have worked there?	• Coffee meetings, online catch-ups, where can I gather relevant touch points and data to underpin my conclusions?
How can I take control of the interview? Do I have enough data for a one-pager?	• Can I take control with a 90-day plan?

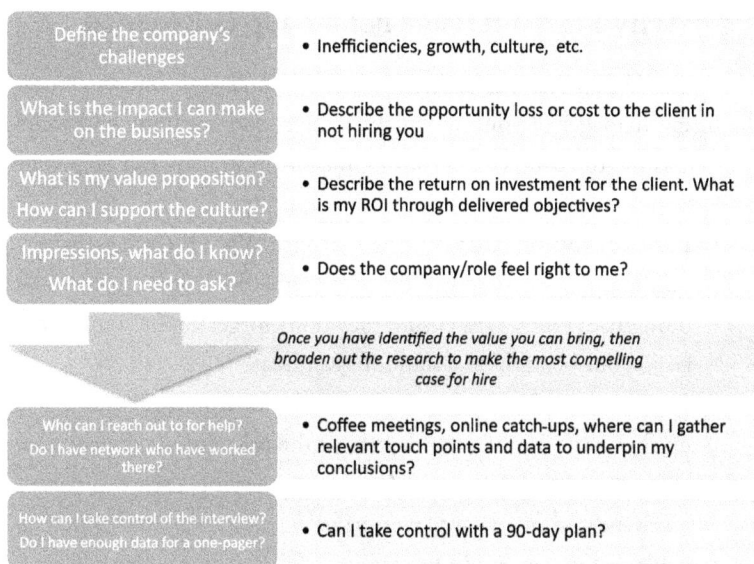

Figure 13.1 Interview analysis template

the moment. Then outline a roadmap taking you from where you are now to securing an offer for the role. Ask yourself:

- How are you feeling about the opportunity, is it still right for you? Assuming it is, what can you do now to make sure you are seen to be the most proactive and suitable candidate?
- What are you nervous about? What can you address now, what can you learn later?
- What are the specific challenges that the company is facing and why are you uniquely qualified?
- What are the measurements of success, and what do you bring to the table to execute on these?
- Shape your experiences and achievements into a statement or document showing intent and process. Hone this statement to be sharp, concise, and compelling.
- Submit and use within the next conversation, or suggest a follow-up, to take control by using your document to guide the discussion and to further corroborate your learnings.

Why Post-Interview Follow-Up Is Essential

After the interview, your goal should be to reinforce your interest, remind the hiring manager of your key qualifications, and continue positioning yourself as the top candidate. A strong follow-up strategy can help you:

- **Position Top of Mind**: Hiring managers often interview many candidates, it's easy to get lost in the mix. Well-timed and thoughtful follow-ups ensure they don't forget about you, solidifying your position as a standout candidate.
- **Demonstrate Professionalism and Commitment**: Following up shows that you are serious about the role and understand the importance of clear communication, conveying a sense of commitment that many employers value.
- **Address Unanswered Questions**: A follow-up can give you the chance to address any questions you didn't fully answer or elaborate on during the interview. This also demonstrates that you are thinking creatively and proactively about the role and its challenges.
- **Take Ownership**: Instead of waiting for a decision, post-interview strategies allow you to keep momentum, signaling to the employer that you are proactive and capable of driving initiative-based outcomes, qualities important in many roles, especially leadership or management positions.

The 90-Day Plan

This is a powerful tool for candidates in an interview process as it demonstrates foresight, strategic thinking, and a proactive approach to the role. Presenting such a plan shows that the candidate has done their homework, understands the company's challenges, and is already envisioning how they can contribute from day one. In broad terms a 90-day plan is a one-pager that outlines proposed, specific, actions and goals for the first 30, 60, and 90 days, of any role. The plan is designed to show how the candidate will integrate into the organization, build relationships, learn the business, and start delivering measurable results.

Suggested Timing

I would not be looking to produce a 90-day plan until you have assessed the opportunity and the company you are interviewing for. This is to ensure that you understand the drivers, ambitions, and culture of the company you are looking to join. Knowing the hiring process and who is part of your interview panel is also a vital thing to have considered. You should especially know whether a session with your potential hiring manager will come around after a first interview with them, or if they are available to check in with you as you progress. You should be targeting to get a version of your 90-day plan or a directional one-pager to them, once you are through at least two of your panel interviews.

If the opportunity is one you have manufactured through networking in the connected job market, your interview process could be less formally set out. In the drifting scenario I mentioned, I had a clear sense of what and how I could contribute, but, for whatever reason, the deal was not closing. It was at this point I put across a one-pager, not a 90-Day plan, but a hybrid of the two. The moment I shifted the discussion from hypothetical to practical, with time-based actions and financial outcomes, then the pace changed considerably. Within a day I had an offer and, soon after that, a contract. This is what I mean about seizing the initiative and shaping a conversation toward the outcomes you are looking for.

Creating the Perfect 90-Day Plan

The baseline is that you have thoroughly researched the company and role on offer.

- **Ensure You Ask Questions:** Designed to open points you can address your skillsets toward. Ensure you are taking full advantage of the opportunity and making the most of the chance to question each interviewer on your journey to uncover what is being sought for this role. Each perspective and insight will build your case. With a clear sense of what is at stake, what the priorities and focuses are, and what challenges are present, you will be better able to shape a 90-day plan to hit and deliver the points you need.

- **Phase the Plan:** Think about the journey you will undertake as you join this company. Try always to position actions in terms of your impact and focuses. Make sure that your language is simple, to the point, and clearly articulates your priorities and the outcomes you will deliver.
- **Example Focuses:** These need to be true to your environment and authentic to you, make sure they are also very much matched to tangible outcomes for your role.
    - **First 30 Days:** Learn the products, understand the go-to-market (no matter what your function), immerse yourself in company culture, understand key processes, build relationships, and gather data on performance indicators.
    - **Next 30 Days (60-Day Mark):** Transition to contribution, taking on responsibilities, implementing initiatives, and offering insights. Build reporting and hiring plans.
    - **Final 30 Days (90-Day Mark):** Deliver measurable results. Lead projects, optimize processes, and drive meaningful impact with measurable outcomes. Review and focus on the next quarter.

Always:

- **Set SMART Goals:** Ensure objectives are Specific, Measurable, Achievable, Relevant, and Time-bound to highlight clear milestones and progress tracking.
- **Align with Company Objectives:** Make sure your plan aligns with the company's, or your hiring manager's broader goals and strategy, proving that you are not just focused on personal success but also on contributing to the organization's overall achievement.
- **Show Flexibility:** While a 90-day plan should be concrete, highlight your ability to adapt and respond to new information or evolving priorities. Review and assessment should be built into the plan. This shows you can pivot if needed.
- **Emphasize Collaboration:** Outline how you will work with key stakeholders and build relationships across departments to create synergy and foster teamwork.

- **Incorporate Quick Wins:** Identify early wins you can achieve, which will show immediate value and help build momentum in your role.

90-Day Plan Template

It is important to keep the 90-day plan (Figure 13.2) elevated, simple, and clear. Do not spell out the detail. This can be discussed in face-to-face sessions. Revisit it often and use the resultant inputs and outcomes to keep this functional as a living document, as once you are in the role, the benefits do not end there. A 90-day plan serves several uses. First, in setting yourself some guardrails, you are putting your commitment and time toward certain key activities linked to outcomes. By creating and sharing the plan, you are also holding yourself to be accountable to timelines and deliverables.

The window of opportunity in your first 3 to 6 months in a business is quite tight. One can easily head in multiple directions that serve the short-term and do not set you or your business up for sustained success. A 90-day plan will help to focus your mind on what is most important, what can be ignored, and what help you will need to achieve identified quick wins as you lay down the foundations for a more concerted executable plan.

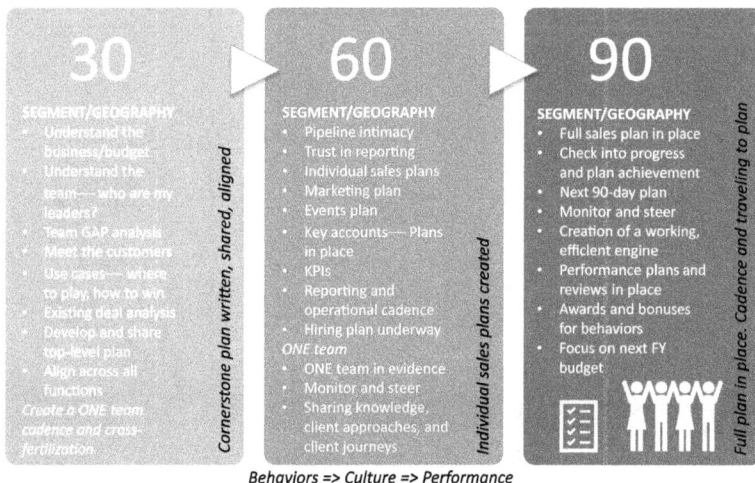

Figure 13.2 90-day plan template

Interim One-Pagers

If your 90-day plan is not yet fully formed, at least have a one-pager indicating something of your approach, deliverables, and focuses, aligned to the values and asks of the business. A more general version could best be described as an insight into *"How did I get here and how will I get there?"* (Figure 13.3)

This one-pager outlines basic focuses and approaches that you might undertake when entering a business for the first time, shaped by your past, showing:

- Approach to Role.
- Expectations in Role.
- Where You Will Focus.
- What Will You Bring.
- What You Need to Win.

Of course, you could develop other layers to this, and always it is best to bring yourself to any approach like this, making it authentically your own, shaped to your present and unique circumstances. This document

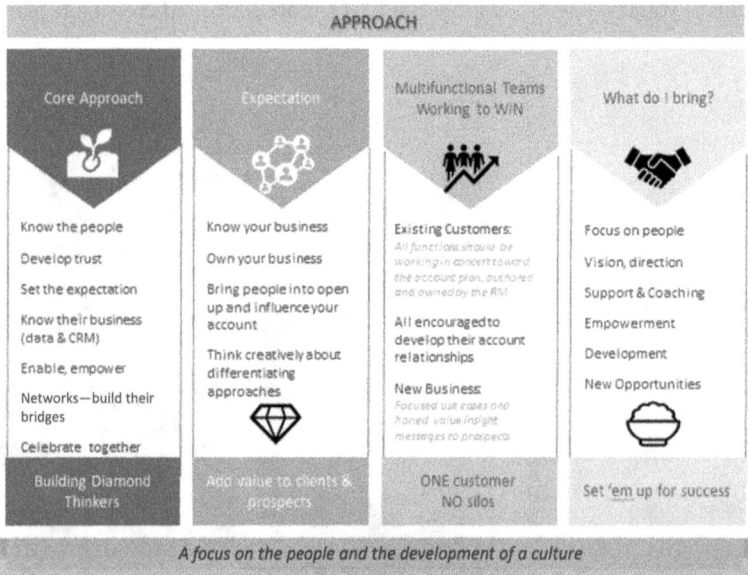

APPROACH			
Core Approach	Expectation	Multifunctional Teams Working to WIN	What do I bring?
Know the people	Know your business	Existing Customers: *All functions should be working in concert toward the account plan, owned by the RM*	Focus on people
Develop trust	Own your business		Vision, direction
Set the expectation	Bring people into open up and influence your account		Support & Coaching
Know their business (data & CRM)		All encouraged to develop their account relationships	Empowerment
Enable, empower	Think creatively about differentiating approaches		Development
Networks—build their bridges		New Business: *Focused use cases and honed value insight messages to prospects*	New Opportunities
Celebrate together			
Building Diamond Thinkers	Add value to clients & prospects	ONE customer NO silos	Set 'em up for success
A focus on the people and the development of a culture			

Figure 13.3 *How did I get here and how will I get there?*

shows initiative, preparation, and a strong desire to contribute. It can show your core approach and philosophies. A one-pager demonstrates ownership by showing you have thought strategically about how to contribute to the organization. It provides tangible value by showcasing your process, problem-solving skills, and strategic thinking tailored to the company's needs. You want to signal that you have thoroughly researched the role and company, setting you apart as proactive, innovative, and genuinely invested in making an impact going beyond the typical follow-up notes.

A Word About Accuracy

Putting yourself out there is inherently a risk, and it does take some confidence to do it. This is why the majority of candidates play it safe at the end of the day. It is also why these folks do not get hired or promoted as quickly as others. I want you to be confident in what you do not and cannot know at this stage of a process. 70 to 80 percent accuracy is good enough. Consider the benefits in terms of differentiating from other candidates through developing fact-based conversations about the actions you would take in the business, while building a springboard to an effective start to your time in role. Focus on what you have learned through the lens of what you do know, especially around the outcomes you know you can deliver.

I do want to highlight the power of actively using your network. You will be surprised how many will help, provided that you come prepared and make the ask in a compelling manner. I have turned down job opportunities based on feedback outside of the hiring process. You can never have enough insight and data when making a critical decision. You should be aiming for better, deeper conversations and, believe me, this is exactly what the interviewers want also.

Timing and Delivery

Timing is critical when submitting your follow-up materials.

- **Immediate Follow-Up:** Send a thank-you email within 24 hours of your interview. This email should be concise, expressing gratitude for the opportunity and briefly reiterating your excitement for the role.

- **One-Pager:** Within 48 to 72 hours of the second or third interview. In your email, explain that you have given more thought to the position and wanted to share some strategic ideas on how you would contribute to the role, to be discussed further.
- **Check-Ins:** If you haven't heard back within an expected period, send a polite follow-up email. Reiterate your continued interest and ask if any additional information is needed to help move the process forward.

Suggested email wordings:

"Dear [hiring manager,]
I trust you are well. I very much appreciate the time the team and you have taken out to bring me through the interview process for the [name of role] so far. In our interview, we discussed [company name]'s current priorities and challenges, particularly in the areas of [specific areas mentioned in the interview]. I am excited about the opportunity to contribute to the team and have prepared a 90-day roadmap for how I would approach the role of [position title]. I have paid particular attention to [your defined approaches] which enabled me to transform my previous function in the following ways [list achievements in bullet points]. I would love to hone this further and would like to discuss where I can focus for the greatest outcomes for the business, either at the next [scheduled interview date and time] or, alternatively, at your convenience.
Best [your name]"

More Advanced Approaches: The "Cornerstone"

For senior leaders, you can of course adapt the supporting document you use to focus on deeper topics. "The Cornerstone" (Figure 13.4) is a vision statement used to fuse people to a mission. I covered this in my last book, *"The Cultural Sales Leader: Sustaining People, Attaining Results."* Be careful when you use the cornerstone as it is a more strategic document in nature. You may want to focus on more basic executional topics initially.

PLAN

2024 AMBITION — **20 NEW CLIENTS** — **LAND and EXPAND**
- Conversions to full rollout
- Upselling and Cross sells

$+25% Growth — $1,800m TTV 2024 — $800m net profit 2024

YOUR LOGO

VISION

To be recognized as the go-to enabler of flexible and mobile work arrangements globally, allowing for fast deployment of world-class talent, seamless contractor engagement, smoother onboarding, timesheet to payroll and financing, while increasing efficiencies and misclassifications.

"The one-stop global workplace enabler that makes you unstoppable"

STRATEGY

FOCUS AND FINISH LAND AND EXPAND
- Define Market and key opportunities
- Laser focus on the deals that matter (new logo and existing customers)
- Revenue now
- Build pipeline to drive development and investment

WINNING TECHNOLOGY
- Regional voice; technology accessibility and optionality as a competitive strength
- Understanding the localized support needed to deliver pilots and develop long-term coauthored projects

FLAWLESS EXECUTION
- Focus on continually improving go-to-market effectiveness in collaboration with adjacent functions
- Grow a superior product capability across our businesses

INVEST IN OUR PEOPLE
- Become a consistent employer of choice
- Build an ability to develop, attract, motivate, and grow tomorrow's talent

Revenue at +25 percent growth | Develop customer stories/use cases | People behaviors | Adjust plans

MISSION

- Lead from the front
  - Build and develop team
- Focus and finish (New business)
  - Define the use cases
  - Define the country markets
  - Prioritize the largest, most profitable prospects and deals
- Land and expand (Key accounts)
  - Develop strategic plans to penetrate and protect all strategic clients
- Understand the needs of customers and partners

VALUES

- We make it our own
- We make it better
- We succeed together
- We create magic!

BEHAVIOURS

Inspire high standards while showing we care
- People-first
- Expect excellence

Build bridges to win
- Act across the business to win
  - Work across all functions
  - Be the voice of the region/market
- Grow smart

Shape our markets and adapt to rapid change
- See around corners
- Know the customer

Be a talent multiplier
- Grow self
- Grow people
- Identify and develop talent
- Adopt individual personal development plans tied to annual review

PRIORITIES

Meet/develop/build team
Understand pipeline
  ➤ Transfer wins/opportunities across regions
Define the key opportunities/priorities
  ➤ Focus activities to plan
  ➤ Build the use cases

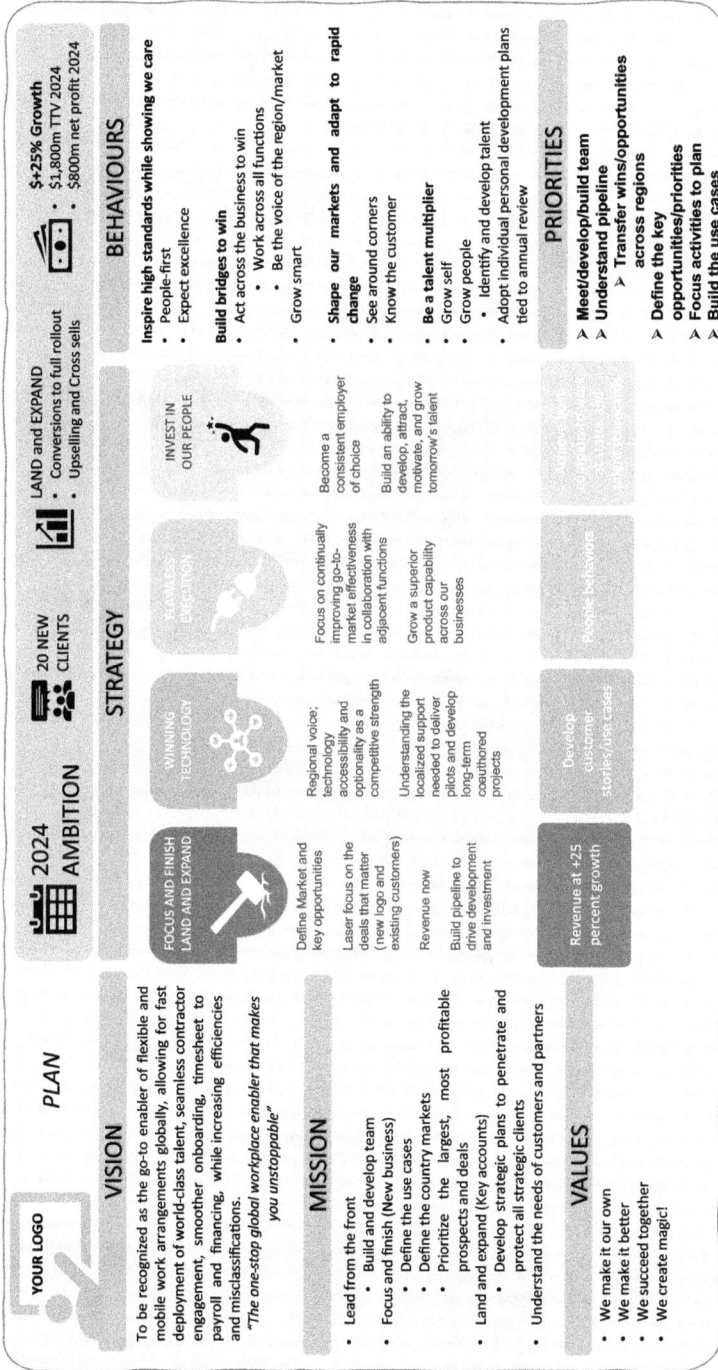

Figure 13.4 Cornerstone strategic overview template example

Additional Tips

Make these documents look as if you already work at the company, this is a subtle way of signaling that you belong. Using the company website, you should be able to find logos and PowerPoint (.ppt) file formats that you can use as if you are already an employee. You can also use SlideShare. If you cannot find these resources, then keep your slides clean and uncluttered. Clean is better than colorful in this respect.

Talking Yourself Out of a Role

A word to the wise. I have been the recipient of outreach that goes too far and that reflects badly on the candidate. Natural enthusiasm and confidence on the candidate side can boil over sometimes becoming lengthy, overly passionate, questioning, and even antagonistic. To be clear, this is not going to help you win roles, frankly, these behaviors will have the opposite effect. They also demonstrate a lack of EQ. So, be mindful always in terms of the impression you are likely to make and always defer to being professional, clear, and concise in anything you submit to the hiring panel. To be an effective salesperson, you must elevate and be clear about delivered value. Bring simplicity to your outreach, less is more. Remember that you will speak to points in more detail in person and that you do not have to provide detail at this stage.

- Never be aggressive.
- Do not outstay your welcome, never badger or harass.
- Be clear and concise in anything you send to hiring managers.

Takeaways

- *Sometimes you need to force the agenda and move the selection process along.*
- *Use 90-day plans or other one-pagers to highlight your value to the hiring company and where your proposed focuses and results will be.*
- *Do not worry about what you do not know. These documents are supposed to trigger deeper conversation and to invite coaching so that you might be successful in role.*

CHAPTER 14

Showcasing Your Cultural Fit

Chapter Summary

- Increasingly, effective company culture is recognized as being transformational to team and company results.
- Find the hiring company's mission, values, and leadership style prior to interview and prepare your stories to match these.
- Discover what stage the company culture is at, is it in transformation, fully realized, or failing? What role can you play to bring the culture to life?

Cultural Fit

Product, approaches, methods, and skills can all be taught, but attitude and cultural fit is everything.

Richard Cogswell, *The Cultural Sales Leader: Sustaining People, Attaining Results.* Copyright © Business Expert Press, LLC, 2024

Company culture refers to the shared values, beliefs, practices, and behaviors that define how employees interact, working together to conduct business within an organization. It encompasses everything from the company's mission and goals to its workplace environment, communication style, leadership approach, and also office norms like dress code or work hours. It's the "personality" of the company that influences the day-to-day experience of employees. A strong company culture promotes a sense of belonging, motivates, and aligns employee actions with the company vision. As a candidate, company culture can significantly affect your decision to join an organization and your potential for success there. If a company's culture aligns with your personal values, work style, and career goals, you are more likely to feel comfortable, motivated, and engaged.

For instance, if you thrive in a collaborative, innovative environment, but the culture is rigid and hierarchical, you may find it difficult to fit in or perform at your best. Assessing the culture during interview is crucial to ensuring long-term job satisfaction and growth. Understanding the lived priorities of your hiring manager and senior company leadership is therefore a serious element of the due diligence you should be performing on any company you interview for.

Increasingly, hiring managers are also hiring for what could be termed as, "cultural fit." For example, I have on several occasions been involved in turnaround situations at companies. This requires clear communication to everyone about the mission and specific goals of transformation, alongside a clear articulation and lived experience of the behaviors needed to build the new culture and drive results.

Having identified team members I would build around, I would always include them in the interview processes for new hires, with a focus on fit for the role and fit for the culture. If the team bought into the candidate as much as I did, then I knew the group would gel, support, and help shape the person coming in. Bringing in someone who might clash with a carefully curated and managed culture can be highly disruptive. Be attuned therefore to what is important to your hiring manager.

If you can discover the specific focuses and goals for the team you are joining, then you have all you need to understand how the mission fuses to the people element. These are then critical topics to both question and dig into during interview. You should also focus on practically demonstrating how you can integrate into this environment and, importantly, how you can contribute to improving it. At the end of the day, company cultures and smooth-running teams are fragile. Unless they are invested in and protected, they can decline and sometimes even die. As such, great leaders will be focused on this issue, as they know full well that they are only ever one bad hire, or headhunter away from a retention issue.

Demonstrating Your Cultural Fit

Here's how to best demonstrate your cultural compatibility to a prospective company:

- **Research the Culture in Advance:** Understanding the company's culture is foundational to demonstrating compatibility. Prior to interview, research the organization's mission statement, values, and work environment. The more you know about the company's culture, the better you will be able to tailor your answers to show that you are a natural fit. Do not be afraid of leaders who honestly state that the culture is not yet there or that there are issues. If they are focused on the topic and support you in demonstrating the behaviors that foster culture and drive results, this is the key. This already sets the stage for a meaningful conversation that can help differentiate you in interview.

- **Highlight Shared Values:** Throughout the interview, make sure to emphasize how your own values align with the company's. Employers want to know that you are not just applying for a job, but that you are genuinely passionate about what the company stands for. Expressing enthusiasm for the company's mission and long-term vision can leave a strong impression. Explain why their purpose resonates with you personally and how it aligns with your career aspirations. Mirror your language, written and presented, for example. If the company values collaboration and teamwork, curate your interview stories to highlight where you have collaborated or been involved in highly team-focused environments to attain great outcomes and results. Use the company's core values as a backdrop to shape your responses to behavioral questions and be specific about how those values resonate with your personal and professional life. Speaking to your personal values and philosophies can be powerful, doing so demonstrates that you have thoughtfully considered how you align with the company beyond just your technical skills.

- **Ask Culture-Focused Questions:** Toward the end of the interview, when you are invited to ask questions, take the opportunity to delve into cultural aspects of the company. Ask thoughtful questions such as "*How would you describe the company culture here?*" "*What qualities do successful employees share at this organization?*" Such questions signal to the interviewer that you are serious about finding a cultural fit and that you are genuinely interested in being part of the company's community. It also gives you further insight into whether this company is the right place for you to grow. If the interviewer suggests that there are issues, then use this opportunity to dig deeper and ask how your contribution can help the direction. Again, this is an excellent opportunity to shape the conversation toward your qualities and experience in similar or adjacent environments.

When culture and talent align, it creates the ideal match for both the candidate and the employer.

Takeaways

- *Be sure to find out about the company culture and leadership style prior to and during the interview.*
- *Think about how your values, philosophies, and practical experiences might show behaviors and outcomes that the hiring company and manager may need or value.*
- *Incorporate cultural alignment into your responses and approach to curating your stories for interview.*

CHAPTER 15

Optimizing Your Personal Brand

Chapter Summary

- Building a personal brand involves intentionally shaping and managing the way others find and perceive you, both online and offline.
- Define your unique proposition based on your personal passions, values, and philosophies.
- Showcase skills, achievements, and expertise through social media creating brand consistency.

Your personal brand is defined by the impression you leave behind.

Building a personal brand assumes that you have bought into the principle that you have to put yourself, your attributes, and your experiences into the shop window to be recognized by potential employers. Authenticity and consistency are key. Here are some steps you can take to build and enhance your personal brand. This boils down to consistently giving something of yourself, your values, and your principles.

The more progressed you are in your career, the more likely you will have come to know yourself better. You will have worn the scars and victories of your personal journey and received much conducive feedback along the way. You will have adapted and learned from those around you, as much as from your direct experiences. You should have a sense of your core motivations, your values, approaches, and perhaps even a philosophy in terms of your role and function. If you are not entirely there, or beginning to shape and define these, take time now to think about this as part of your growth journey. By showing these traits, you will gain more followership, you will also come across as more attractive to potential employers. These are great elements to play to when networking, creating a professional online presence, and to build your interview stories around. They will lend credibility to your candidacy and will help to separate you from the pack.

Development of Your Personal Brand

Think of three statements to describe your working style, for example:

- **Strategic and Goal Driven:** *Setting clear and measurable goals for the team, developing sales strategies that align with the overall business objectives, and focusing on key performance indicators, while guiding the team to achieve targets through well-versed tactics and plans.*
- **Coach and Mentor:** *Prioritizing the development of team members and the provision of ongoing coaching and feedback to enhance individual and collective performance.*
- **Customer Obsessed and Relationship Driven:** *Focusing on prioritizing customer needs by building long-term, mutually beneficial relationships through active listening and fostering effective communication, all aimed at delivering value to clients.*

If you are struggling to craft appropriate statements, do not write them straight away. Instead think of what values and attributes you hold dear and how you manifest these:

Values

1. **Family:** My family comes first. I strive to maintain strong, loving relationships.
2. **Integrity:** I believe in honesty, transparency, and ethical behaviors in all aspects of life.
3. **Growth:** I value personal and professional growth, I am curious and look for opportunities to develop. I seek uncomfortable situations to progress this journey and my learning.

4. **Empathy:** I aim to understand and support others' emotions and perspectives.
5. **Community:** I aim to make positive impacts and to serve my community.
6. **Health:** Physical and mental health is an important driver for me.

Attributes

1. **Team Player:** I work well together within a team and seek diverse, divergent, and even challenging perspectives and contributions.
2. **Curious:** I am interested in those around me and in new ideas, approaches, and experiences.
3. **Patience:** I approach situations with calmness and understanding, even in testing circumstances.
4. **Coaching Mentality:** I do not seek to provide solutions for others, rather, I mentor them in helping them find their own solutions for their better and more confident development.
5. **Reliability:** Others can count on me to be consistent and supportive always.
6. **Unbiased:** I spend my time and energies wisely and seek all inputs and contributions.
7. **Creative:** I push myself to find creative and innovative approaches.
8. **Resilient:** I react well to change and nebulous situations, seeking the positives and opportunities for growth.

These lists are not comprehensive, so do take time to think of what best describes your unique make up. Do not shy away from any that you might find or consider to be negative or current weaknesses either. Be honest. If you are still unsure, ask for feedback from others about how you show up. Asking for feedback is a highly vulnerable position to put yourself in. Be prepared to be gracious for all the feedback you receive. If the feedback you receive is not so good, then treat all inputs as genuine gifts, especially if you have been blind to the traits described. All feedback, and especially those on areas to improve, is to be treasured. A fine resource on this topic comes from Dr. Tasha Eurich. Her book, *Insight: The Surprising Truth about How Others See Us, How We See Ourselves, and Why the Answers*

Matter More than We Think (Copyright © 2018), explores the importance of self-awareness and feedback in achieving success and fulfillment.

The building blocks of creating a personal brand might be considered as follows:

- **Self-reflection:** Identifying values, strengths, and passions. Determining your long-term goals and what you want to be known for.
- **Defining Your Niche:** Determine your experience and what sets you apart from others. Go on to find who is your target audience and tailor your messages accordingly.
- **Create a Personal Mission Statement:** Craft a concise and compelling statement that reflects your values, goals, unique qualities, and, in time, your philosophy. This can be a powerful tool to help you focus, stand out, and more effectively market yourself to secure the job that best fits your values and goals.
- **Professional Image:** Ensure that your image aligns with your personal brand and is authentic.
- **Online Presence:** Establish a strong online presence through social media platforms, a personal website, or blog. Ensure to optimize your LinkedIn profile with a professional photo, a compelling headline, optimized search terms, and a detailed summary. Consider LinkedIn posting to develop your professional voice and to share your experiences and opinions.
- **Consistent Branding:** Use a consistent tone and style across your platforms. Ensure you are aligning to your offline activities as well.
- **Content Creation:** Share valuable content related to your niche and make sure to comment on other's posts. Write blogs, create videos, or share posts and insights on social media to showcase your expertise. Monitor your online presence regularly. Respond to comments and feedback professionally.
- **Networking**: Attend industry events, conferences, and networking functions. Connect with others in your field and engage in meaningful conversations with them. Actively seek mentors, peers, and other professionals.
- **Skills Development:** Make it a mission to continuously learn and stay updated on industry trends, take time to also reflect

on your learned experiences, and learn to listen to yourself and whatever emotions you may be feeling as an important data input.

- **Be Genuine, Honest, and Authentic:** Make sure you are coming from an authentic place that truly reflects who you are as an individual. Make sure you highlight your weaknesses also.
- **Feedback and Adaptability:** Seek feedback from peers, mentors or those you trust. Be open about adopting constructive feedback to evolve your personal brand.
- **Evaluate and Adjust:** Much of social media is about trying and failing and trying again. Adjust as you need to.

Building a personal brand is an ongoing process, and consistency and authenticity are key. Regularly revisit and refine your brand to ensure it aligns with your evolving goals and aspirations.

Initial Steps Toward Brand Building

Consider this a journey. The initial step is to clean up your LinkedIn profile and ensure that it reflects you and tells your professional story. Then you can interrogate your values and find your branding statements, these will change over time as will the stories that underpin this journey exhibiting your growth.

Find Your Passions

- **What is your passion?**
  - Your mission statement or philosophy. A paragraph or short set of bullet points that best describe you. Think in terms of an elevator pitch. What would you say that passionately conveys an essence of yourself if you had no more than a minute with someone you were keen to impress?
- **What are you best at, and what got you into your industry?**
  - What has been your journey? The best presenters, salespeople, and speakers can convey their concepts through storytelling. What are your stories? Why are these important?

- **Why did you get into your field? Chance or design? If chance, did you learn to love it?**
  - When did the light bulb turn on for you? Has it always been there? Why? If it came later, at what moment did you reflect you had become an expert in what you do? If you are new to work or aiming for a dream role, what motivates you and how do you see the role you are going for?
- **What have you learned that you would pass onto others?**
  - What would you say to your younger self? How have you helped develop those around you? How would you, if given the chance, manage a task or function and why?
  - There is no shame in failures. When and how have you failed? What did you learn and how have you effected change? How does this relate to the role you are going for?
- **What do you dislike?**
  - Dislikes can help you find your strengths and passions. Identifying what you are in opposition to is a powerful viewpoint to come from.
- **Accomplishments**
  - No better way to demonstrate capability than through your successes. These could be stories from other fields, experiences, or life in general, provided they have some bearing or insight in terms of your capacity to grow in the role you are applying for.
- **What is your work philosophy?**
  - What makes for a successful person in your function?
  - What experiences taught you about your role, how might you manage others, and what are processes that work and why?
  - Who influenced you and why? Professionally or personally. Who are your role models and why?

Building Your Mission Statement

A well-crafted personal mission statement is a powerful tool in your job search and career development. It provides clarity, helping you to stand out, anchoring you, boosting your confidence, aligning you to the right employers, and supporting your professional growth. By articulating your unique value proposition and career aspirations, you can more effectively market yourself and secure the job opportunities that best fit your goals, aspirations, and values. It is also a step to defining your core beliefs or philosophy around what it is that you do.

The statement should reflect your core values, strengths, career goals, and philosophies toward role or function and should also reflect what you can offer to a potential employer. Here is a proposed approach to creating this important baseline. To begin with, go back to those three statements from the beginning of the chapter.

Assess Your Strengths and Skills

Consider your key strengths and skills. Think about what you do best and what makes you stand out. These could be technical skills, soft skills, or a combination that is unique to you.

Clarify Your Goals

Define short-term and long-term career goals. Ask yourself, what do you want to achieve in your career? What roles or industries are you targeting? Where do you want to see yourself in 3 to 5 years' time? It is ok if you do not yet have a total sense of this. Reflect and review this regularly and flesh out your plan as you develop your experiences and thoughts on the matter.

Understand Your Unique Proposition or Value

Determine what qualifies you for the role you are seeking and what you bring to the table. This could be a combination of your experiences, skills, personality traits, and accomplishments. This becomes even more powerful if you can think in terms of an ROI. The hiring company is going to expend resources on hiring you and will pay and incentivize you. What are the tangible business outcomes you are going to land in terms of efficiencies, process improvements, cost savings, revenue, or new horizons built?

Structuring Your Mission Statement

Now you should be ready to craft your mission statement. Aim for clarity and brevity, one or two sentences at most. Think of it as your concise expression of purpose, similar to your company's "why" or value proposition. Write it so anyone can immediately understand what you strive to achieve, avoiding jargon or industry-specific terms. Focus on your target audience. Make sure to tailor to resonate with the types of employers and industries that you are targeting. Consider what they value most in potential colleagues. Start with a few drafts, do not worry about making it perfect. This will need honing and adaptation as you head on your journey. Focus on getting your ideas down for now, then edit and refine, cut unnecessary words or cumbersome statements, and focus on resonating with impact and memorability. An effective way to help hone the message is to gain feedback from trusted colleagues, friends, or mentors.

Example Mission Statement

[Who you are] + [Why you do what you do] +
[How you do what you do] + [The value that you bring]

- **Marketing Professional Example:** *As a passionate and innovative professional, I thrive on creating compelling campaigns that connect with audiences and drive business growth. My mission is to leverage my creativity and strategic thinking to help companies build strong brands and connect meaningfully with their customers.*
- **Software Developer:** *I am a dedicated software developer with a love for solving complex problems and building efficient, user-friendly applications. My mission is to use my technical skills and collaborative spirit to develop innovative solutions that address the needs of the market through accessibility and driving technological advancement.*
- **Project Manager:** *As an experienced project manager, I excel in leading cross-functional teams to deliver projects on time and within budget. My mission is to combine my organizational and leadership*

abilities to ensure successful project outcomes and drive continuous improvement for the mutual benefit of customers and the overall business.

It is best to always be authentic, specific, and positive in your statement so that you might best highlight your brand most effectively. Use for your LinkedIn introduction, your CV, and as your core structure when thinking about how to present your capabilities and when answering interview-based questions. Self-awareness, knowing what motivates you, where your strengths lie, and where you need to grow, is vital. Whether you're navigating your next career move or simply committed to self-improvement, these are the insights that shape your progress. Having developed your mission statement and identified your values, attributes, skills, and achievements, consider these additional exercises to uncover learnings and insights into your drivers.

Me, We, and Work

Going a step deeper, this is an exercise in showing how critical aspects of your life show up as dimensions of who you are and how they interconnect. This helps to determine your core values and drivers, allowing you to set goals and priorities into each area. There is also a clearly cultural aspect to this exercise. Another benefit of this technique is in helping to set balanced and fulfilling life goals, encompassing "me," "we," and "work."

Me

- **Personal Values:** List the core values, beliefs, and principles that guide your life and matter the most to you.
  - Examples: Integrity, health, growth, and creativity.
- **Personal Goals:** Outline short and long-term goals, which could be related to well-being, hobbies, personal and professional development, and anything important to you as an individual.
  - Examples: Achieve work-life balance, run a marathon, or learn a musical instrument.

We

- **Relationships:** Identify key relationships and connections in your life. This can include family, friends, and other meaningful relationships.
  - Examples: Strengthen bond with family, nurture relationships, and build a supportive social network.
- **Community Involvement:** Mention community projects, causes, or commitments that are important to you. This could be charitable support, mentoring you undertake within your network, volunteering, sports, or coaching.
  - Examples: Supporting a charity, volunteer coaching, and giving back to your network.
- **Team:** Mention what you aspire to see within your professional teams.

Work

- **Career:** List the values and principles that guide your professional life. What matters most in work-related decisions?
  - Examples: Innovation, leadership, and work-life balance.
- **Professional Goals:** Specify your career goals and aspirations.
  - Example: Promotion or achievement of defined milestones.
- **Skills Development:** Mention the skills you want to acquire or develop, improve, or learn.
  - Example: Enhanced leadership skills, improved public speaking, and developing mentoring skills.
- **Work-Life Balance:** Highlight how you aim to balance professional and personal to achieve overall well-being.
  - Example: Set boundaries.

Letter to My Future Self

Now that you have considered what has got you here and what your current makeup is, consider where you want to be. Writing a letter to your future self can be a powerful and reflective exercise. It allows you to set goals, express your current thoughts and emotions, it also offers a snapshot of where you are now, alongside the journey you'll look back on when you eventually read it.

1. *Choose a Future Date*: As with all exercises, making it time-bound is part of the commitment. It could be a year, 3 years, or longer. Make sure this is a meaningful timeframe for you.
2. *Current-State Reflections*: What key events and experiences are happening? Reflect on your achievements, challenges, and personal growth to this point.
3. *Set Intentions*: What will you hope to have accomplished by the time you open the letter? Outline aspirations, personal and professional. Include specific goals as well as broader themes and values.
4. *Write Your Letter*: Start with a friendly greeting and encouraging tone. Address yourself as if a close friend. Share your thoughts and your feelings and be openly honest and vulnerable. Discuss hopes and dreams as well as future expectations. Express gratitude and be thankful for the experiences that have shaped you.
5. *Keep It Personal*: You are writing this for yourself and your journey, make it yours.
6. *Seal and Store the Letter*: Store the letter "to my future self" and remind yourself to review this when the time comes.
7. *Open and Reflect*: Take the time to reflect on your past and on your thoughts and intentions. Compare this state to your current one and see how you have grown and changed. Be kind to yourself and reward your bravery.

Focusing on Yourself as Part of Your Job Hunt

It is too easy to know aspects of yourself without ever really isolating them, unpacking them fully, and analyzing why they may or may not be holding you back. These exercises ensure that you are taking responsibility for your growth journey as you shape your approaches to hiring managers as part of an ongoing and sustainably winning proposition. Acknowledge your weaknesses as well. Remaining curious and open to learning is a part of helping to drive your own self-growth as well as improving your chances to get the roles that you desire and deserve.

Above all else and beyond differentiation, these focuses and exercises are about ensuring that you both serve and promote your authentic self. People are at their most effective when in environments of psychological safety, whereby they can go about their work, grow and develop as individuals while being true to their values and beliefs. These processes ensure that you do not compromise on these elements within your job search.

Takeaways

- *Knowing yourself better will enhance your online presence, your CV, and your approaches to hiring companies.*
- *Curate and shape your mission statement through your values, attributes, skills, and accomplishments. Include interrogation of your weaknesses and highlighted areas for development also.*
- *Use your mission statement to highlight your unique value proposition to employers.*
- *Review, improve, and adapt as you grow as a professional, to reflect your developing skillsets and philosophy toward your role and industry.*

CHAPTER 16

Ageism and the Stigma of Being Perceived as "Overqualified"

Chapter Summary

- Ageism is overlooked in discussions about workplace diversity, leaving an important demographic out of the conversation.
- Be aware of the challenges of seeking work later in your career, particularly if sideways moves or moves that might be perceived to be below your competency.
- Do not let your CV do the talking. Break the recruitment cycle and challenge rejections.
- Think of how you can present yourself to mitigate beliefs and concerns that might confront your application.
- Propose the concept of "Returnship," being asked back and being fully present as a guiding force for coaching.

We Need to Talk About Ageism

It is time to address ageism, which remains a stubborn and often unaddressed bias in the workplace. Despite the growing recognition of race, gender, and disability as critical aspects of workplace diversity, age as a demographic is often overlooked or undervalued. This oversight not only undermines efforts to build truly inclusive work environments, but also ignores the significant contributions of older workers, who bring a wealth of experience, skills, and perspective to organizations.

I have come across numerous posts on this topic on LinkedIn. One I recently commented on came from a recruiter. She shared a story about a senior candidate with years of experience and leadership titles applying for a smaller role. Her point was that when a candidate seems overqualified, it should prompt a conversation to understand their motivations and how they perceive the position. She's absolutely right, but the reality is, this kind of dialogue is not happening. As you might expect, posts like this generate a lot of engagement, some even suggest that a junior recruiter might hesitate to meet with a senior leader fearing they won't be able to control the conversation. The problem is that this issue will only become more prevalent, driven by demographic shifts and societal changes.

Surely being "overqualified" is good, no? Surely hiring a person with experience or skills beyond the job spec would be an absolute win. You would think all these things, however, that is not how these interactions play out. Senior and mature candidates are being ignored, or worse, simply rejected without any kind of conversation, and this rejection usually comes with a meaningless statement such as, "*Thank you for your application. We were extremely impressed with your [qualifications or skills], however, we feel you are overqualified for the position on offer.*" In this circumstance, the recruiter is saying "no" outright, "no" to meeting you, "no" to trying to understand your motivations and goals, and "no" to your application.

Career Extension

Studies, surveys, and economic reports consistently reveal that people are retiring later than in the past and that this trend is most acutely observed in developed countries across the world.

- **OECD Data**: According to the Organisation for Economic Co-operation and Development (OECD), labor force participation rates among older individuals (aged 55+) have increased significantly over the past few decades. In the 1980s and 1990s, early retirement was more common, but more recently, there has been a notable trend toward delayed retirement.
  - In 2000, about 47 percent of people aged 55 to 64 were still in the labor force. By 2020, that figure had risen to about 63 percent across OECD countries.

- ○ The participation rate for those aged 65+ also increased, with countries like the United States, Japan, and South Korea leading in the percentage of older people who stay employed.

Sources: OECD.org

Increased Average Retirement Age

- **U.S. Data (Bureau of Labor Statistics):**
  - ○ In 1990, the average retirement age in the United States was about 62 years. By 2020, this had increased to 64 for men and 62 for women.
  - ○ The percentage of people aged 65 to 74 who are still working has been steadily increasing. In 2000, about 19 percent of this age group remained in the workforce. By 2020, this had risen to over 26 percent.
  - ○ Projections from the Bureau of Labor Statistics estimate that by 2030, approximately 32 percent of people aged 65 to 74 will still be working, and 12 percent of those aged 75 and older will remain employed.
  - ○ In Germany, the retirement age is gradually increasing to 67.
  - ○ France recently raised its retirement age from 62 to 64, sparking significant public debate and protests.
  - ○ In the UK, the retirement age for state pensions is increasing and is expected to reach 67 by 2028 and 68 in subsequent years.
  - ○ Japan: Known for having one of the highest life expectancies, mandatory retirement age rose from 60 to 65 and companies are encouraged to keep workers employed beyond 65.

Source: www.biz.gov

Welcome to the new norms. People are simply living longer and healthier lives, which has extended the average working lifespan, resulting in older individuals choosing or needing to stay in the workforce for financial or personal fulfillment reasons. To illustrate this further, in 1980, the average life expectancy in the United States was about 73 years, compared to 79 years in 2020. Similar trends are seen in most developed nations. This longevity has contributed to the need for more savings and income during retirement, encouraging later workforce exit.

Financial Drivers

The issue of financial necessity is a very real driver. Pensions, retirement funds, personal savings, and social security systems may not provide enough income for some, leading to longer careers. Many older workers continue working past traditional retirement age due to concerns about saving enough for retirement. Many countries are extending official retirement ages to support their aging populations and balance pension funds. Data from the U.S. Federal Reserve's 2019 Survey of Consumer Finances found that the median retirement savings for people aged 65 to 74 was only US$164,000, which is far below what is required for a comfortable retirement.

Staying Active

Retirement is no longer viewed as a hard stop but rather a flexible transition. Many choose to work part-time or in different roles for personal fulfillment, to remain mentally and socially active, or to pursue passion projects in later life.

"Overqualified"

Despite these strengths, older workers face pervasive barriers in recruitment. One of the most frequent and frustrating challenges older workers encounter during the job search process is being labeled as "overqualified." This is often an unsubtle way of dismissing their applications without addressing age bias directly. Employers cite concerns such as:

- **Cost Assumptions:** Employers may assume that older workers will demand higher salaries or benefits due to their experience.
- **Retention:** The thought might be that someone with experience and qualifications might seek to move onto something more

fitting than a junior role, should one come along. Some recruiters also assume older workers are nearing retirement and thus are not a long-term investment.

- **Concerns about Cultural Fit:** The perception might be that a senior worker might not align well into a culture of younger, tech-savvy dynamism and entrepreneurialism, or will resist adapting to new workplace norms.
- **Motivation:** The concern might be that an "overqualified" individual might be bored or demotivated in a more junior role.
- **Reporting Lines and Dynamics:** In many organizations, there are no systems of mentorship at all, second, some leaders might be concerned about managing or leading a worker with more qualifications and experience than themselves.
- **Skill Misconceptions:** Despite evidence to the contrary, older candidates are sometimes perceived as out of touch with modern technology or lacking up-to-date skills.

Such biases can prevent organizations from benefiting from the value older workers offer. Older workers aged 50 and above are an indispensable asset to the workforce. Statistics consistently prove the unique qualities and contributions of this demographic, which run counter to perceptions or concerns within the recruitment industry.

Experience and Expertise

Workers over 50 typically have decades of experience in their industries. This depth of knowledge enables them to mentor younger employees, navigate complex challenges, and make informed decisions. Studies by AARP* reveal that 87 percent of employers find older workers to be more reliable and knowledgeable compared to their younger counterparts.

*Source; AARP.com

Stability and Commitment

Older employees are less likely to job-hop, offering organizations greater stability and reduced turnover costs. According to the U.S. Bureau of

Labor Statistics, workers aged 55 and older stay at jobs three times longer than those aged 25 to 34.

Source; US Bureau of Statistics Employee Tenure Summary September 26, 2024.

Strong Work Ethic and Adaptability

The stereotype of older workers being resistant to change is increasingly debunked. Research shows that experienced employees are not only eager to learn but often excel in adapting to technological advancements when provided with training opportunities.

Enhanced Emotional Intelligence (EQ)

Decades of interpersonal experience equip older workers with heightened EQ, which is invaluable in leadership roles, conflict resolution, and fostering team collaboration.

The Ignored Value of Older Workers

According to an AARP survey, 61 percent of workers over 45 have experienced or witnessed age-related discrimination during their careers, with recruitment being one of the most common settings for this bias. Moreover, a study by the Federal Reserve Bank of San Francisco found that job applicants aged 50 to 64 are 46 percent less likely to receive a callback than those aged 29 to 31. All of the above could be easily investigated and resolved if the candidate was interviewed based upon their motivations and reasons for seeking the role they have applied for. There are a number of troubling aspects to this:

- **You can only ever rise?** As you gain experience on your career progression, it is typical to be promoted and then to be identified for more senior roles. You climb the corporate mountain, but as you climb you cannot branch out so easily, as if you try and traverse sideways as opposed to higher, you might fall entirely. But why can't someone for personal reasons or work-life balance concerns take a less stressful or involved role? The linear mindset of professional growth assumes that career development always involves moving "upward" in terms of responsibility, authority, and compensation. As a result, when senior executives seek to downsize into less demanding roles later in their careers, recruiters may perceive this as a red flag, questioning their motivation, commitment, or potential to stay engaged. These factors create challenges for mature executives who wish to step back without stepping out of the workforce entirely.

Impact on Workplace Inclusion

Failing to embrace age as a dimension of diversity undermines workplace inclusion in several ways:

- **Missed Opportunities for Knowledge Sharing:** A lack of intergenerational diversity deprives teams of the chance to blend innovative ideas from younger workers with the strategic foresight of seasoned employees.
- **Reinforced Stereotypes:** Overlooking older workers perpetuates damaging stereotypes, marginalizing a significant portion of the population.
- **Widening Skills Gaps:** Ignoring experienced workers exacerbates skills shortages, particularly in sectors requiring leadership, mentorship, and specialized expertise.

A Path Forward

Organizations must take proactive steps to combat ageism and leverage the strengths of older workers. Strategies include:

- **Reframing Recruitment Practices:** Banning phrases like "overqualified" from recruitment language. Instead, emphasize the value of expertise and seek roles that align with the candidate's skills. Implement blind hiring practices to reduce unconscious age bias during résumé screening.

- **Promoting Lifelong Learning:** Provide opportunities for older workers to upskill or reskill, particularly in technology and emerging fields. Recognize and reward continuous learning efforts, demonstrating that growth is valued at all stages of a career.
- **Building Age-Inclusive Cultures:** Include age diversity in hiring strategies and set measurable goals for hiring and retaining older employees. Foster intergenerational collaboration through mentorship programs and teambuilding initiatives.
- **Educating Leadership and HR:** Train managers and recruiters to eliminate age-related biases. Highlight the business case for age diversity, emphasizing its link to innovation, employee engagement, and improved customer understanding.

By dismissing older workers as "overqualified" or irrelevant, organizations miss the immense value they bring. Recognizing age as a key dimension of diversity requires a shift in mindset, to viewing older employees as vital contributors to organizational success.

Mitigation and Persistence

If you are knowingly overqualified for a role or a senior worker applying for a position, it is crucial to address potential concerns proactively during the application process. Know that employers may worry about issues like salary expectations, cultural fit, or long-term commitment. The first thing you should do is always apply directly to hiring managers, and not through HR, (until they change). Here are other techniques to position yourself as a strong candidate:

Tailor Your Résumé and Cover Letter

- **Focus on Relevance:** Highlight skills and experiences directly related to the job you are applying for, rather than including every senior-level achievement. This keeps your application aligned with the role and avoids overwhelming hiring managers.
- **Simplify Titles:** If your previous titles sound intimidating (e.g. "Senior Vice President") consider using functional titles

that reflect your experience without overshadowing the position (e.g. "Department Manager.")

- **Emphasize Collaboration:** Showcase your ability to work with diverse teams and adapt to varying organizational levels, reducing fears of potential rigidity or a "command-and-control" mindset.

Address Concerns in Cover Letters

- **Acknowledge Your Experience:** Without overemphasizing your qualifications, recognize that you bring significant expertise and explain why you're excited about this specific role. For example: *"While my experience may extend beyond the role's requirements, I'm eager to contribute my skills to [specific team/project] and grow alongside the company."*
- **Show Alignment with the Role:** Clarify how the position fits into your career goals, emphasizing passion, stability, or a desire to focus on meaningful work. For instance: *"This role allows me to leverage my strengths in [specific area] while continuing to make a tangible impact in [industry/field]."*
- **Reassure on Long-Term Commitment:** Mention your interest in the company's mission and culture, signaling that you are not just passing through.

Adapt Your Interview Approach

- **Emphasize Flexibility and Humility:** Demonstrate willingness to learn, adapt, and collaborate. Avoid appearing dominant or overly qualified by showing genuine enthusiasm for being part of a team.
- **Communicate Aligned Goals:** Be prepared to discuss why the role aligns with your career objectives without seeming like it's a "step down." You might say: *"I see this as an opportunity to bring my expertise to a role where I can make an impact and focus on [specific aspect of the job]."*
- **Reassure on Authority Dynamics:** Assure the interviewer you respect and will support leadership, avoiding any perception of undermining managers who may have less experience.

Compensation Concerns

- **Clarify Salary Flexibility:** If the employer assumes you expect a higher salary, make it clear you are open to compensation aligned with the role. For example: *"I'm confident we can find a mutually beneficial arrangement that works for both of us."*
- **Avoid Undervaluing Yourself:** While showing flexibility, ensure you don't undersell your value. Reassure them that your interest is not purely financial but also tied to the role's impact and alignment with your goals.

Highlight Mentorship and Team Contributions

- **Offer to Mentor:** Position your experience as an asset to the team by offering to mentor younger colleagues or junior team members, displaying how you can enhance team development.
- **Promote Team Collaboration:** Emphasize your track record of fostering team success and adapting to diverse workplace environments, which can counter fears of being overbearing.

Build Relationships Early

- **Network Strategically:** Leverage professional networks to secure referrals. A recommendation from someone within the company can help address any preconceived concerns about your qualifications.
- **Informal Interviews:** Use informal conversations to learn about the company's culture and hiring preferences, giving you a chance to tailor your application accordingly.

Reframe Overqualification as a Strength

- **Confidence, Not Arrogance:** Acknowledge your experience as a value-add rather than a liability. For example: *"I bring a wealth of experience that allows me to hit the ground running and deliver* *results quickly, while staying open to learning and adapting to the company's unique needs."*

- **Stress Enthusiasm for the Role:** Make it clear that you are applying because you genuinely want the position, not because you are settling or desperate.

Be Transparent About Career Transitions

If this role represents a shift in focus or a downshift in responsibilities, be upfront. Explain why this is the right move for you at this point in your career, whether for better work-life balance, a passion for the field, or a desire to focus on specific skill sets.

Prepare for Objections

Anticipate concerns about overqualification and address them confidently during the interview. For instance: *"I understand you may have concerns about my experience, but I'm committed to bringing my skills to this role while aligning with the company's goals."*

By proactively addressing potential concerns and emphasizing your value in a way that aligns with the employer's needs, you can successfully overcome the "overqualified" label and position yourself as a strong, desirable candidate.

Persistence

If you are facing challenges, one strategy could be to take the employer head on. Use all the techniques and suggestions contained to not take no for an answer while finding out the real reason for the rejection. Do be conscious of the true "openness" of the job posting and recruitment process though, perhaps there is someone already shortlisted. To get to that clarity, you must rejoin the conversation and potentially network yourself around the recruiter. A polite rejoinder could be to raise the concern that your motivations and potential contributions are not being heard, backed by research into the company's values, goals, and mission.

"Returnships"

Some organizations are leading the way on the issue, as exceptions to the rule. A Returnship is a call for an ex-employee, a mature worker in this case, to come back to an organization and to plug back into the emails, calls, and meetings as a mentoring force. Hopefully, a trend that will become mainstream over time.

Takeaways

- *Be aware that ageism and a reaction to your experience and acquired skills could be an issue if you are looking for smaller or sideways moves later in your career.*
- *Consider ways to show your motivations for application early.*
- *Do not take the recruitment process as your only avenue into a dialogue with the company and look at ways to confront any lazy rejections.*
- *Ask about "Returnships."*

Conclusion

Your Personalized Recruitment Revolution

Always be, passionate, compelling, and succinct. Add value and never outstay your welcome.

In his commercial life, my father worked for one employer his whole working life. Interestingly I have recently seen two of my network who have also enjoyed long-term work anniversaries. One, a dear friend of mine, Brian, has, at the time of writing, just celebrated his 27th year at the same company. Such tenure is becoming increasingly rare.

For the majority, tenure at companies is measured in a handful of years before we seek or move to the next opportunity. Rapid technological advancements have accelerated the pace of change in many industries, requiring workers to frequently update their skills, often leading to job displacement. Furthermore, modern workers, particularly younger generations, tend to prioritize career growth, diverse experiences, and work-life balance over long-term job security, leading to higher job mobility. This combination of technological, economic, and cultural shifts has made long tenure less common.

All of this can result in an environment where talent is seeking new opportunity more often, but also where unforeseen situations can hit us out of nowhere. The economy, the job market, and the recruitment industry are all disinterested when it comes to good talent in a hurry. What I frequently see is that people in this situation have often not had their networks optimized. A merger, an acquisition, a change of direction, cost-cutting measures, all result in good people suddenly coming to terms with being on the job market and needing to find a solution in a hurry.

Change the Game. Change Your Results

In today's hypercompetitive job market, it is no longer enough to navigate the traditional recruitment processes or conventional HR gatekeepers. The key lies in prioritizing direct engagement with hiring decision-makers. Achieving this requires a paradigm shift, embracing the art of self-promotion, developing a personal brand, and strategically networking to uncover and create opportunities. Success in today's job market belongs to those willing to play a different game than the one presented to us. Those who adapt, innovate, and take charge of their career trajectories with confidence and intentionality will create better results for themselves.

My Connected Job Market Story

Let's check back in with my connected job market story. The next step was another informal coffee meeting with a senior member of the team. Imagine that in a "normal" hiring process, do you think you would be invited to meet one of the hiring panel over a coffee or a drink?

Be prepared in these processes for different types of meetings or, at the very least, be prepared for the unexpected. You can be forgiven for thinking that you have been introduced to someone as a "straight interview." This may not be the case at all. You could well find yourself being sized up for your interpretation of a situation. Make sure you note all the verbal clues you have been given along the way. This is why after any discussion it is wise to take a moment to run through everything you spoke about and to make some notes. In respect to my situation, the hiring manager had made it plain that he wanted the new leader to make their own choices and assessments. So, when you are introduced to others, prepare for both an interview and potentially other dynamics.

The gentleman I met was well presented with many years of service in the company, clearly someone who knew the landscape, the challenges, and the ways to forge success. He asked me how I came to be a part of the process, which led into my recounting some perspectives I had about the role, including where I could see myself fitting in. He then told me his perspectives which were completely different to mine!

I was initially perplexed. I knew now that whatever I said, outside of questions, would bring me into a contrasted position with the person opposite me. Still, I wanted to test some of my assumptions and see how they landed.

As my position was one of having competed with this company for over 6 years, I was keen not to offend, so I caveated my points by saying that these were the perspectives of someone outside looking into an environment where I saw all the tools and capabilities to dominate in the market. As I anticipated, I noticed a shift in body language as I shared my observations, both the strengths and shortcomings, about potential vulnerabilities or opportunities to capture market share. I got the sense that he didn't view my insights as entirely welcome.

Leaving the meeting, I felt it was quite possible that I had ended my journey. I messaged the hiring manager and gave him my summary. The response was that I was going to hear different perspectives on what the role required, but that change-focused business leadership was critical. I was still in it. I had learned a great deal. It looked as though whoever was to take the role would have some work to do to communicate a clear strategic aim and would need to effect change. It was also clear that some restructuring might also be required. This is where a connected job market process can be so different to a normal interview process. Here I was already getting inputs to the style of my prospective boss, the issues on the ground, and the challenges the role would offer. All of this now becomes material for you to assess and make decisions on. This includes a reflection on whether a role is right for you or not.

When meeting across an interview panel it is okay to be confused or to pick up that other perspectives or viewpoints exist within the organization you are interviewing for. I remember another panel interview for a company needing a change of direction. Out of four interviews I was left totally confused by one, where the described challenges and focuses were radically different to those the other leaders had spoken to. As it turned out, this person was part of the previous management and had perspectives that were not aligned to the current expectations for the part of the business I would be running. It was up to me to draw these conclusions and to align those with the leaders I would be reporting to. Those who represented change.

Not All Connected Job Market Engagements Lead to an Outcome

At the time of writing this book, I am reminded of the many conversations I am having within my network. The one relayed above may well come to nothing, but I hope it illustrates the nature and dynamic of the connected job market. There is no way I would get through a normal recruitment process to apply to this company. I guarantee HR, their ATS, or connected recruiters, would have discarded my application long ago. Yet I am still very much involved and can call the hiring manager anytime and set up a meeting. I have bypassed HR and can continue to identify the value I could bring to this organization. By reframing yourself as a resource rather than an applicant, you elevate your approach from simply seeking employment to demonstrating your capacity to drive impact, thereby positioning yourself as an indispensable solution to the hiring manager's needs.

To stand out in today's competitive job market, particularly amid the volume of LinkedIn applications, it is essential to bypass traditional gatekeepers such as generalist HR professionals and talent recruiters. By proactively engaging in direct conversations with hiring managers and clearly demonstrating your potential ROI in role, you not only increase your chances of being hired but also position yourself to shape the recruitment process in your favor. This approach not only helps you make a stronger, more personalized case for yourself, but also enables you to navigate the hiring landscape with greater control and success.

Today's recruitment process can feel like navigating a maze, with algorithms and overwhelming competition often standing in the way of your goals. There is a better way. By tapping into the power of the "connected job market," and displaying your value, you can bypass traditional hurdles and open doors to the opportunities you deserve. Support and smarter approaches are out there, you just need to take the first step toward harnessing your unique value and ensuring that the right people get to discover that with you.

About the Author

Richard Cogswell is a people-first sales leader. He is an organizational team builder who believes that people, vision, values, and behaviors build winning sales cultures. Richard has held multiple senior sales leadership positions within several industries, working across EMEA, the United States, and APAC, within startups and listed multinational companies, including a stint with one of the world's largest recruitment firms. Other books by Richard include the Axiom Business book of the year 2025 gold medalist, *The Cultural Sales Leader: Sustaining People, Attaining Results*.

You can find out more from Richard at www.richardcogswell.com.

Index

www.ingramcontent.com/pod-product-compliance
Lightning Source LLC
Chambersburg PA
CBHW061153220326
41599CB00025B/4472